After Aztlan

After Aztlan

LATINO POETS OF THE NINETIES

▲ ▼ ▲ ▼ ▲ ▼ ▲ ▼ ▲ ▼ ▲ ▼ ▲ ▼

edited by Ray González

David R. Godine, Publisher
Boston

First published in 1992 by
David R. Godine, Publisher, Inc
Horticultural Hall
300 Massachusetts Avenue
Boston, Massachusetts 02115

Library of Congress Cataloging-in-Publication Data
After Aztlan : Latino poets of the nineties / edited by Ray González.
    p. cm.
    Includes bibliographical data.
    ISBN 0-87923-931-X (HC) ; ISBN 0-87923-932-8 (SC)
    1. American poetry—Hispanic American authors. 2. American
poetry—20th century. 3. Hispanic Americans—Poetry.   I. González,
Ray.
PS591.H58A69   1992   92-7960   CIP
811'.54080868—dc20

Second printing, 1994
Printed in the United States of America

This book is for Óscar Zeta Acosta, Pablo Neruda, Rubén Salazar, Julia Canales, and for El Paso, which refuses to erode into the dust of the desert.

Contents

Introduction

After Aztlan gathers some of the best contemporary Chicano and Puerto Rican poets writing in the United States today. Their work portrays the current state of Latino writing and shows that these writers have created a complex, vibrant literature. They come from varied backgrounds, but their diverse voices share the common concerns of all Latino writers—finding ways to overcome political barriers placed upon them, preserving the traditions of a culture that stresses close familial ties, and most of all, showing how Hispanic literature has become a true part of "mainstream" American arts and letters.

The contributors of this anthology contributed to the evolution of Hispanic literature through their commitment to the form of poetry, their national accomplishments beyond initial publication in small presses, and their prolific body of work during a period when multicultural literature and writers enjoy their largest audience and readership. As poets coming into their own in the eighties and nineties, they have gone beyond the earlier notoriety of Chicano and Puerto Rican literature of the sixties and seventies, when political chaos and social change first brought together the work of Latinos, African Americans, and Native Americans.

Today's Latino writers are sustaining the legacy of this coalition and of authors such as Alurista, Ricardo Sanchez, Lalo Delgado, Oscar Zeta Acosta, José Montoya, and other poets and activists of the sixties who were some of the first writers to present alternatives to the established literary canon of this country. By writing poems and stories straight out of the barrio, reciting their work before mass rallies, and photocopying poetry pamphlets in editions of several thousand, these earlier poets influenced Latino writers who would take off in the midseventies.

These earlier writers also helped to shape and define the concept of Aztlan, an edenic ideal adopted from Aztec mythology, forming it to envision a North American continent free of agression in which native people could flourish and shape their own culture and literature. The search for this idealistic state of Aztlan reached its peak in the early seventies. As more Latinos gained social power, the drive to create a unique identity free of oppression evolved into artistic assimilation for these writers, a successful recognition and place for multicultural writing. The many gains that have been made by Latinos over the last twenty years have come with a more realistic approach to living in America with all its racial problems. For Puerto Ricans, this political concept has been different from Chicano ideals. Their struggle for independence from the United States continues to this day and the preservation of their island culture remains a priority for them. Together, these poets not only represent literary goals that have been reached over the last two decades, but their poems also symbolize the triumph of their native cultures.

The fact that half of the contributors in this collection are women sheds light on the powerful development of Latina writers since those exciting times. Over the last twenty years, Latino literature has gained a larger audience due to the success of many of its women writers, and these writers have led the way in taking this literature from its earlier stance, entrenched in political rhetoric, to a more rounded, diverse vision.

As a result, Latino poetry contains every crucial aspect of this culture, combined with the mature vision of its writers, regardless of genre. These poets display the sharp political focus needed to confront change at the turn of the century, but they also bring a mastery of craft, syntax, and voice needed to take poetic forms into new territory. Latino poets writing today have learned the lessons of the sixties, and as artists, chart their own direction without rhetoric and posturing. They write about social injustice from a position of power, not from wishful thinking. This is poetry of the most potent kind, spoken by voices that anticipate what lies ahead, as well as what still needs to be done. This is poetry *after* Aztlan—poetry that carries the struggle of its people with the individual vision of the poet, achieving more than any political speech because the social and personal myths of these writers are powerful forces that rise from undeniable survival instincts.

As Americans of all cultures look back, they can't help but acknowledge the ways in which the accomplishments and mistakes of their ancestors placed them where they are today. We are all shaped by family history, bounded by ongoing social restrictions, and left to come to terms with our past. Latino poets, perhaps more than other American poets, write a great deal about family and how past events are the true spiritual forces that need to be understood and overcome. Some of the most moving and disturbing poems in this book deal with family, and show the ways in which a poetic vision can be an extension of these blood roots. By confronting the past, these poets learn how their ancestors survived to pass on similar lessons to later generations. These poems also debate the value of preserving ancient traditions and beliefs, ways of life that may no longer serve a need in today's world. On closer reading, however, the poems that most deeply question family history are often the same ones that embrace events of the past in order to find a new way for the next generation. These voices are shaping Latino poetry into a universal language that all readers can understand.

The poets in this book are writing in a time when the richness of American poetry is being celebrated on many levels. They were selected for the quality of their writing and for what they have to say to us all. This collection of poems rises out of a great momentum, continuing the legacy of a literature that has been written by many voices, perpetuating one of the oldest characteristics of American letters.

Ray González, 1992

After Aztlan

Francisco Alarcón

In a Neighborhood in Los Angeles

I learned
Spanish
from my grandma

mijito
don't cry
she'd tell me

on the mornings
my parents
would leave

to work
at the fish
canneries

my grandma
would chat
with chairs

sing them
old
songs

dance
waltzes with them
in the kitchen

when she'd say
niño barrigón
she'd laugh

with my grandma
I learned
to count clouds

to point out
in flowerpots
mint leaves

my grandma
wore moons
on her dress

Mexico's mountains
deserts
ocean

in her eyes
I'd see them
in her braids

I'd touch them
in her voice
smell them

one day
I was told:
she went far away

but still
I feel her
with me

whispering
in my ear
mijito

Prayer

I want a god
as my accomplice
who spends nights
in houses
of ill repute
and gets up late
on Saturdays

a god
who whistles
through the streets
and trembles
before the lips
of his lover

a god
who waits in line
at the entrance
of movie houses
and likes to drink
café au lait

a god
who spits
blood from
tuberculosis
and doesn't even have
enough for the bus

a god
knocked
unconscious
by the billy club
of a policeman
at a demonstration

a god
who pisses
out of fear
before the flaring
electrodes
of torture

a god
who hurts
to the last
bone
and bites the air
in pain

a jobless god
a striking god
a hungry god
a fugitive god

an exiled god
an enraged god

a god
who longs
from jail
for a change
in the order
of things

I want a
more godlike
god

My Hair

when
you met me
my hair was
black like
the blackest
canvas

with your hair
I'll make the finest
paintbrushes
you would tell me
biting
my ears

and I would run
with my black
hair loose
like a colt
its black mane
shining

with your gray hair
I've made now
a long rope
you tell me
wrapping it
around my neck

Letter to America

pardon
the lag
in writing you

we were left
with few
letters

in your home
we were cast
as rugs

sometimes
on walls
though we

were almost
always
on floors

we served
you as
a table

a lamp
a mirror
a toy

if anything
we made
you laugh

in your kitchen
we became
another pan

even now
as a shadow
you use us

you fear us
you yell at us
you hate us

you shoot us
you mourn us
you deny us

and despise
everything
we

continue
being
us

America
understand
once and for all:

we are
the insides
of your body

our faces
reflect
your future

Jimmy Santiago Baca

Bells

Bells. The word gongs my skull . . .
Mama carried me out, just born,
swaddled in hospital blanket,
from St. Vincent's in Santa Fe.
Into the evening, still drowsed
with uterine darkness,
my fingertips purple with new life,
cathedral bells splashed
into my blood, plunging iron hulls
into my pulse waves. Cathedral steeples,
amplified brooding, sonorous bells,
through narrow cobbled streets, bricked patios,
rose trellis'd windows,
red-tiled Spanish rooftops, bells
beat my name, "Santiago! Santiago!"
Burning my name in black-frosted streets,
bell sounds curved and gonged deep,
ungiving, full-bellowed beats of iron on iron,
shuddering pavement Mama walked,
quivering thick stainless panes, creaking
plaza shop doors, beating its gruff thuds
down alleys and dirt
passageways, past men waiting in doorways
of strange houses. Mama carried me past
peacocks and chickens, past the miraculous
stairwell winding into the choirloft, touted
in tourist brouchures, "Not one nail was used

to build this, it clings tenaciously
together by pure prayer power, a spiraling
pinnacle of faith . . ." And years later,
when I would do something wrong,
in kind reprimand Mama would say,
"You were born of bells, more than my womb,
they speak to you in dreams.
Ay, Mejito,
you are such a dreamer!"

Fall

Somber hue diffused on everything.
        Each creature, each emptied corn stalk,
        is richly bundled in mellow light.
In that open unharvested field of my own life,
I have fathered small joys and memories.
My heart was once a lover's swing that creaked in wind
of these calm fall days.
Autumn chants my visions to sleep,
and travels me back into a night
when I could touch stars and believe in myself . . .

Along the way, grief broke me,
        my faith became hardened dirt
        walked over by too many people.
My heart now, as I walk down this dirt road,
on this calm fall day,
        is a dented
        tin bucket
        filled with fruits

picked long ago.
It's getting harder
to lug the heavy bucket.
I spill a memory on the ground,
it gleams,
rain on hot embers
of yellow grass.

Day's Blood

I toss yesterday's tortillas
to pack dogs at my door—
with bared fangs and smoldering
matted scruff-fur hackles,
they grunt-scarf then slouch away.
Snouts in weeds for more chance scraps,
in mournful whines and whimpers, heel-nipping,
with floppy, sagging, lopsided shuffle,
they cross fields towards the Oñate Feedmill,
where they gnaw hooves and snarl
over gutted intestines
at the back door of the slaughterhouse.
At night they sleep in the Rio Grande bosque,
and walking there myself at night,
in the moonlight,
I've seen their eyes glint in the brush,
bloody obsidian knife blades
dripping with the day's blood.

At Night

I lie in bed
and hear the soft throb of water
surging through the ditch,
from extreme to extreme water bounds,
clumsy country boy,
stumbling over fallen logs and rubber tires
to meet a lover
who awaits in her parent's house, window open.

As I used to for love.

Now gray-black hair,
vigorous cheeks, weathered brow, chapped lips,
dismal thoughtful eyes,
I float in brown melancholy on the lazy currents
of memory, studying my reflection
on the water this night,
with distant devotion,
a swimmer who has forgotten how to swim.

Cordelia Candelaria

Teenage Son

Staring at a slip of winter sunrise

At a cool red ball reluctantly ascending
I am stopped by the moment,

> the world's teetering balance
> between heavy pendant gray
> and fuzzy swelling peach

A blink of eyelids
I'm still staring
But I've missed the movement:
The darkness vacuumed into orange daybirth
Day sounds day creatures daylife filling.

> When did you become a frog?

Killers

The paper's merciless in reminding us
who shares the planet with our averageness.
They frighten and fascinate.
We have to read their stories.
We have to keep them in front of us
assaulting someone else, tearing her lingerie

to newsprint shreds, shooting his left ventricle
precisely. You wonder what they do. How
they live their lives. Up early? Late?
Flowered sheets? Jam on their toast?
When it rains like tonight heavy and cold
do they sit cozy somewhere
reading poems or writing them or plotting how
to kill you couplets of murder, cups of rum
in front of a snug fire somewhere
warming toes, making small talk, marking time.

Refuse of Our Teeming Shores

You wonder about garbage
about the growing mountains of trash.
Cities produce countries of it
families produce cities of it
and orphans wander alone

Question marks of flesh and blood
punctuating the urban landscape
like forgotten trees in corners
of El Greco paintings.

A boy I know
was forgotten by his parents.
He lived in a city apartment with Grandma.
After school he walked around the apartments

making cement sidewalks
                    playgrounds of possibility
making lightpoles
                    appletrees of adventure

turning couples arriving from work

                    into lots and lots of parents.

Ana Castillo

Nani Worries About Her Father's Happiness in the Afterlife

He knew nothing about death,
before he died.
None of us did.
Then he died,
and I was left to wonder where he went.

The *Nahuas* sent their loved ones,
accompanied by an *escuinctle*,
to travel for four years
before reaching *Mictlan*:
Region of the Dead,
also called "*Ximoayan*"—
Place of the Fleshness.
Mictlan: The House of *Quetzal* Plumes,
where there is no time.

Jesus descended into Hell
for three days,
freed his predecessor, Adam,
and returned to earth.
Oh—such stories I have heard!
Men and their intentions.
I did not know what to think.

I looked about the room, held his hand,
turning cold in mine,
his mouth open, having gasped
for his last breath of this life.
He was no longer in a sweat.

I wish I knew where he was—
floating above, near the ceiling,
perhaps, like those near-death cases report.

Was he pleased with our Christian
praying over the corpse,
my many kisses on his forehead,
our reluctance to leave him alone?

A cold winter Chicago night:
Ash Wednesday, February 28th.
The uselessness of doctrine in
these times. Ma and I decided
two things with that in mind:

This is hell.
This is not the whole story.

Seduced by Natassja Kinski

I always had a thing for Natassja Kinski.
My Sorbonne clique and I went to see her latest film. Giant
billboards all over Paris: Natassja—legs spread, her
lover's face lost in between.

I watched Paris, Texas twice, living with
the eternal memory of those lips
biting into a fleshy strawberry in Tess.
Thank you, Roman Polanski.

Long after I have gotten over Natassja Kinski,
I am with a Chicago clique on holiday. I am an atom now,
in constant, ungraspable flux, when my Bulgarian scarf is
pulled off my neck. It is Natassja Kinski.

She has removed her KGB black-leather coat; bottom of
the ocean eyes are working me, and yes, that mouth . . .

When we dance, I avoid her gaze.
I am trying every possible way to escape eyes,
mouth, smile, determination, scarf pulling me
closer, cheap wine, strobe light, dinner invitation,
"Come home with me. It's all for fun," she says.

I dance with her friends again. I am a tourist in my
hometown, and the girls are showing me a good time.
I think I'll leave with someone else.
But she finds me at a table in the dark.
"What do you want, my money?" I ask. She reminds, cockily,
that she has more money than I do. I am a poet, everybody
does. And when we dance, I am a strawberry, ripened and
bursting, devoured, and she has won.

We assure each other, the next day, neither of us has
ever done anything like that before.

By Sunday night, we don't go out for dinner as planned.
Instead, over a bottle of champagne,
Natassja wants me forever. Unable to bear that mouth,
sulking, too sad for words, I whisper: *"te llevaré conmigo."*
As if I ever had a choice.

An Ugly Black Dog Named Goya

An ugly black dog named Goya
witnessed through
glass doors
a woman's legs high
on its master's shoulders.
Goya's tongue hung
panting loud.
Her eyes challenged
Goya's, she called out:
¡—Mira *ese perro cochino!*—
Thrust interrupted,
irate master threw a shoe,
dog ducked, dejected
by a slew of insults.

From a corner
locked in shadows
Goya pretended to sleep.
Early gray winter inhaled
late afternoon,
obscuring this one—
nothing like his mistress
who was pale and thin,

nervous as a bitch,
brought him fresh meat,
said gaily: "Here, Goya, baby!"
and who was afraid
of men
passing joints on the street,
waiting for tenants
to leave
so they could enter
back windows,
the mistress who cried
one night: "You can have
this dump! I'm going back
to Forest Hills!"
She always phones
at dusk just
to see if another woman
is there
but by then,
the master alone
at work with paints,
canvas, color, books,
and Wagner,
has stopped yelling
at the dog named Goya
too grotesque with hybridism
not to be mean,
lets him lie
near his feet
until the heaviness of winter
exhales a semblance
of light
and they both get to sleep.

Zoila López

If i were you, Zoila,
i wouldn't be here
in English class
with the disturbed child
who sits in the back
with the husband
who doesn't work.
i wouldn't laugh, Zoila,
if my first winter up north
was without boots
and the only thing to
warm me was the photograph
of Jorgito dressed as a
little indian in white
pajamas and sandals on
Guadalupe's Day, just before
he was killed by a truck
that carried oranges.

i wouldn't bathe, change
my dress, look for work,
hold a pencil upright
after this summer when
the baby ran a high fever
and the hospital people in
that marbles-in-the-mouth
language said, "It's okay.
Take her home."
She died that night.

You'd thought she'd just
stopped crying.

i would die, if i were you,
Zoila, a million deaths at
the end of each nightmarish day
with its miniscule hopes like
snowflakes that melt on one's
teeth and tongue and taste of
nothing.

Rosemary Catacalos

One Man's Family

in memory of Bill Gilmore

There was the Dog Man again today,
bent under his tow sack,
making his daily pilgrimage
along St. Mary's Street
with his rag tied to his forehead,
with his saintly leanness
and his bunch of seven dogs
and his clothes covered with
short smelly hair.
Pauline, the waitress up at
the White House Cafe, says
he used to be a college professor.
In a college. Imagine.
And now he's all the time
with them dogs.
Lets them sleep in the same room
with him. Lets them eat
the same things he eats.
Pauline don't like it.
All them eyes that light up in the dark
like wolves'.

I imagine he carries his mother's
wedding dress around in that filthy sack.
I imagine he takes the dress out on Sundays

and talks to it about the dogs,
the way he might talk to Pauline
if she ever gave him the chance.
About how to him those seven dogs
are seven faithful wives,
seven loaves, seven brothers.
About how those seven snouts bulldozing
through neighborhood garbage and memories
give off a warmth that's just as good
as all the breasts and apple pies and Christmas trees
and books and pipes and slippers
that a man could use on this earth.
But mostly about how they're dogs.
Friends that don't have to be anything else.
About how nothing could be more right
than for a man to live
with what he is willing and able to trust.

A Partial History of Poppies

You plant a border of poppies in my yard, visit
on chilly mornings to keep vigil, mutter that we all
must do something for this world, and I remember
the red ones were sacred to Ceres when she was still
called Demeter and would not give the world back
its corn, color, the warm air that sprouts seeds, until her
child should come back alive from death's trickster food.

Over and over again she found Persephone memoryless
among the shadows, bargained with Hades for the months
that hadn't been swallowed with his dark

kernels: This is how we got spring, the glory
that is left to life in the face of death, the recurring
poppies, our faith in resurrection. Even though the Bible
tells of seeds that fell on stone and so would not grow.

Even so, each spring all of Greece, to the harshest island,
wears an adamant veil of poppies. One bloom, it is said, for
every drop of blood ever shed in a war. Think of it. That
Troy wasn't the beginning or Hitler even close to the end.
That poppies contradict, raising stubborn little fists all
over the world, yellow in Iceland, white in Asia, Latino
American, the Middle East, brown and purple in Africa,
everywhere the famous red. That finally all blood is the same
color, if memory serves correctly.

On Colima Street, it's not yet spring, and there are poppies
sleeping in rusty coffee cans. The old woman
who dampens the seeds each morning is not the grandmother
of the six-year-old who won't speak since her insides were raped
to shreds by her mother's junkie boyfriend. He's another
version of the poppy, another version of ourselves.
And the old woman, the leap of the heart
and eye that imagines her to be the grandmother
who might yet save the child, these too are versions
of the poppy, of Demeter and Guadalupe. And the choice
among versions remains ours, like the borders
where we either meet or come apart,
like everything we do to keep from falling on stone.

The Measure of Light at the Altar
on the Day of the Dead

If you were here you'd photograph this shrine,
wanting to make it stay forever.

Still, I'm thinking, *hermano*, how some
days there just doesn't seem to be enough
to *go* on. It gets hard to remember why we burn
candles for the dead, offer them sugarcane, *copal*,
flowers the color of light. Is it really

for them or more for ourselves, our way
of whistling into the dark we suspect
is there where they watch from the other side
of things? Surely their eyes adjust right
away to whatever light is available.

Whether glare or shadow. No tricks.
We, on the other hand, put bread out for them,
then eat it ourselves. Nibble at the candy
skulls made in their honor and try not to notice
the ones marked with our own names.

Who can blame us? Meanwhile the dead
are much more with us than we allow. Not just
on this day set aside to praise them, but all
the time. It is because of *them*
that everything means so much.

A ten-year-old boy from Poland is writing
a poem about colors. *Pomarancza wyglada jak*
mandarynka soczysta. We translate with difficulty.
Orange looks like a juicy mandarin fruit.
It is because of the dead that

this brings tears to our eyes, a huge
feeling of gratitude. In the same way as the cracked
song of the old man who is downtown every day
with a cane over each arm and a wide hug for every
building on Commerce Street. It is because of the dead.

Finally, this is what we have to go on.
The world must have its reasons.

The Lesson in "A Waltz for Debby"

in memory of Bill Evans

Amazing how this world manages to be all of a piece.
In Beirut an old woman hearing guns that are nothing
like drums pulls her apron up over her head
and wrings the air in entreaty. In La Resurrección,
Guatemala, Mayan Indians in bright handmade cloth
are hung in trees with their wrists slit and left
to die slowly, turning like obscene ornaments

or jungle birds. And on a strait named Juan de Fuca
off the coast of Washington state, a stranger
is within peaceful shouting distance of six whales
rising and falling on the water: the usual

and regular breathing of God. All this has everything
to do with how you wrote "Waltz for Debby" when she
was three and still had a right to believe life
would always come in gentle measures, the swoop and
sweep of a good dream doing what comes naturally.
You knew better but went ahead

anyway. Just as today I balanced in sunlight
with my own three-year-old nieces, clambering around
one of Fuller's dreams become a toy, the joyful
geometry of a dome turned into triple-sided air.
Even if Demetra refused to step where her favorite tree
cast shadows and twice wouldn't pronounce
the name of her missing uncle,

suspecting the pain it would bring out in the open.
Later she was sullen with the weight of it. Her swing
would not fly, though she leaned with all her might
and crazily against gravity. I thought how all the waltzes
in the world wouldn't save her from learning this.

The man watching the whales, meanwhile, may
fear that in a few years there won't be whales
on this coast. Men either, for that matter.
But more he remembers your fingers as wingtips.
Your remains, clear notes phrased with possibility.
And since jazz musicians mostly work nights, how
you were always finding your way in the dark.

With the Conchero Dancers, Mission Espada, July

There is something in all of this. The heat
heavy on us till it might as well be the mesquite
beam the young goat drags to each day's thin
grazing in the courtyard. It might as well be
the babies, fitful in their baskets, in our arms.
Their cries go out alongside the thick smell of *copal*
burning, as we do, in frail clay vases. Xelina,
who is seven and doesn't know the goat will soon
be meat, wants to touch the beginnings
of its horns, buries her trusting fingers
in the tufts on either side of its mouth.
And there is an old woman in black whose days
are a dark slow vine retreating into memory,
even in full sunlight: the middle son lost in Korea,
the comet-eyed cousin in San Luis Potosí
who loaned her gold earrings and died
in childbirth. *Buenos días, el sol como siempre,*
¿no? Sí, señor, the sun as always.

Celebrating the mass, strangers embrace as though
history were more than it is, resume their fanning
with the Sunday bulletin. There will be a *jamaica*
at Cabrini, a parish council meeting Tuesday.
Something in all of this. In the lightning strings
of the mandolins tuned tense as lovers arching
their backs, the unerring summons of a tree

become drum, bare feet hugging limestone, the earth's
bones, plumed crowns flying in light of everything.
This ancient prayer from the high valleys of Mexico,
spinning and spinning for dear life,
this world to be learned by heart.

Lorna Dee Cervantes

A las Gatas

A Bird, Tiny, Mousie, Grumpy, Cat-Eyes, Flaca, Sleepy, Princess y Betty la Boop

We were nine lives, cat claws plunged in
the caterwauling of *la llorona* and the crying saints.
We believed in witches, wild cards, jokers
and the tricksters who lived without it.
Disciples of the pride, we preyed on fury's wing.
We lied. We stole the heart's desire. We never
got a cent, but feral, flew to another side
of glory. We came; this close to dying,
we gunned the engines of our grief, and gained.
Taught to live from hand to mouth, the moratorium
of our lives began at blood's first quickening.
Given to the beck and call so fast, we primed
our lives that instant when we slipped into the gap
between child and man—and slave. We chose
to stay, tough in the fist of our fathers'
mercy. No face cards in our deck, we dealt
the devil back his hand, we scorched the virgin
from our breasts, as the sweat of heat upon us
did not free us, but did not bind us either.
We had the power then, between three worlds,
to fuse our *bruja* pack, our pact to faith, not
in our futures but, in a present we could fix within
the diamond decks minted in our carboned eyes.
We were crystalline, runaway *rucas* on the prowl,
edge of night in our glassy throats, cut of class

in flyaway manes, the blood of oils on our slapped
cheeks, and with bit lips we smiled to
circling owls. No angels, no *novenas*, no past
spirits that we recognized, nobody's business
what we did, we know we earned our freedom,
and we did.

The Levee: Letter to No One

Today I watched a woman by the water
cry. She looked like my mother: red
stretch pants, blue leisure top,
her hair in a middle-aged nest egg.
She wiped her face, her only act
for old tears, slow as left-over piss.
She was there a long, long time,
sitting on the levee, her legs swinging
like a young girl's over sewer spew.
She slapped her cheeks damp.
I wondered what she watched:
blue herons, collapsing and unfolding
in the tules, half-lips of lapping river
foam, the paper of an egret's tail?
Does she notice beauty? Does she notice
the absence of swallows, the knife
of their throats calling out dusk?
Does she notice the temporary
denial of fish, the flit of silver
chains flung from a tern, the drop
of their dive? Funny, we use the sound
slice to imitate the movement

of hunger through wind or waves.
A slice of nothing as nothing
is ever separate in the realm of this
element. Only symmetry harbors loss,
only the fusion of difference
can be wrenched apart, divorced
or distanced from its source.
I walked the levee back both sides
after that. The river is a good place
for this silt and salt, this reservoir,
depository bank for piss
and beauty's flush.

Night Stand

"Onions, lettuce, leeks, broccoli, garlic, cantaloupe, peaches, plums"

The man whose work is hard
slides onto me glistening
as a bass wielding the sheen
I'm mirrored with when
I step out of the bath.
He wears the patch the sun
has x-rayed to his chest.
He's the color of work.
I'm the color of reading.
I hold my *sembrador*
under the august *calabazas*
of his arms. As first
light drifts through gauze
I have eyes the half-wild

know with: half-bitch,
half-wolf; here I am
extraterritorial
in the divisions,
extinctual as a missing
lynx. It's a foreign well
I drag my sullen bucket to—
in a western bar on a frontage
road we recognize the past
and find we have escaped the thing
which in the night would eat us.

We are gouged by the machinery,
we fill the holes with fire.
We pull the pails another sloshing
day up through the cracks in our
overdue finality. He is wearing
hundred dollar shoes, wool slacks,
linen. He's making better money
now filling holes and digging.
A better life for less is lost.

But no one stays.
If the dirt where I was born
still tamped beneath my feet, if
the concrete avalanche of progress
hadn't filled my love and the
rivers of my youth hadn't iced me
into middle age, I might have
stayed. But no.
His touch is like a man's
despite his age. His Moorish
fur, his Saturn eyes, his

sadness says: although he may not
know beyond the suicide of soul
the poor possess, the threshing race
machines, the names of Goerring,
Himmler, Buchenwald, Farben,
and all that written fables
spell for us—this he knows—
Esta gente no entiende nada.

And I—am the way I had intended.
I've come to what I wanted.
And here, writing, wearing
discarded things the dead have
bought and sold: we know.

Drawings: For John Who Said to Write About True Love

> *"If you had enough bad things happen to you as a child you may as well kiss off the rest of your life."*
> —AN ANONYMOUS MENTAL HEALTH WORKER

"The writer. It's a cul-de-sac," you wrote that
winter of our nation's discontent. That first time
I found you, blue marble lying still in the trench, you
staked in waiting for something, anything but the cell of
your small apartment with the fixtures never scrubbed, the
seven great named cats you gassed in the move. *I couldn't
keep them.* You explained so I understood. And what cat
never loved your shell-like ways, the claw of your ready
fingers, *firme* from the rasping of banjos and steady as it

goes from the nose of the hair to the shaking tip. My
favorite tale was of the owl and the pussycat in love in a
china cup cast at sea, or in a flute more brittle, more life-
like and riddled with flair, the exquisite polish of its
gaudy gauze now puzzled with heat cracks, now foamed
opalescent as the single espresso dish you bought from
Goodwill. What ever becomes of the heart our common child
fastened, red silk and golden satin, the gay glitter fallen
from moves, our names with Love written in black felt pen?
Who gets what? Who knows what becomes of the rose you carried
home from Spanish Harlem that morning I sat waiting for the
surgeon's suction. What ever becomes of waiting and wanting,
when the princess isn't ready and the Queen has missed the
boat again? Do you still write those old remarks etched on a
page of Kandinsky's ace letting go? Like: *Lorna meets*
Oliver North and she kicks his butt. The dates are
immaterial to me as salvation or a freer light bending
through stallions in an air gone heavy with underground
tunnels. Do you read me? Is there some library where you'll
find me, smashed on the page of some paper? *Let it go* is my
morning mantra gone blind with the saved backing of a clock,
now dark as an empty womb when I wake, now listening for your
tick or the sound of white walls on a sticky street. Engines
out the window remind me of breathing apparatus at the
breaking of new worlds, the crash and perpetual maligning of
the sand bar where sea lions sawed up logs for a winter
cabin. I dream wood smoke in the morning. I dream the rank
and file of used up chimneys, what that night must have
smelled like, her mussed and toweled positioning, my
ambulance of heart through stopped traffic where you picked
the right corner to tell me: *They think someone murdered*
her. You were there, all right, you were a statue carved
from the stone of your birth. You were patient as a sparrow

under leaf and as calm as the bay those light evenings when I
envisioned you with the fishwife you loved. And yes, I could
have done it then, kissed it off, when the scalpel of a
single star brightened and my world blazed, a dying bulb for
the finger of a socket, like our sunsets on the Cape, fallen
fish blood in snow, the hearts and diamonds we found and left
alone on a New England grave. Why was the summer so long
then? Even now a golden season stumps me and I stamp ants on
the brilliant iced drifts. I walk a steady mile to that
place where you left it, that solid gold band thrown away to
a riptide in a gesture the theatrical love so well. What was
my role? Or did I leave it undelivered when they handed me
the gun of my triggered smiles and taught me to cock it? Did
I play it to the hilt and bleeding, did I plunge in your lap
and wake to find you lonely in a ribbon of breathing tissue?
Does this impudent muscle die? Does love expire? Do eternal
nestings mean much more than a quill gone out or the spit? I
spy the bank of frothed fog fuming with airbrushed pussies on
a pink horizon. I score my shoes with walking. My skill is
losing. It's what we do best, us ducks, us lessons on what
not to do.
                    Thanks for the crack,

                                    you wrote
in my O.E.D. that thirtieth renewal when the summer snapped
and hissed suddenly like a bullet of coal flung from a fire
place or a dumb swallow who dove into the pit for pay. Kiss
her and it's good luck. I palm this lucky trade but the soot
never sells and I never sailed away on a gulf stream that
divides continents from ourselves. But only half of me is
cracked, the other is launched on a wild bob, a buoy,
steadfast in storm. I may sail to Asia or I might waft
aimlessly to Spain where my hemp first dried from the rain.
My messages wring from the line, unanswered, pressed sheets

from an old wash or the impression of a holy thing.
But don't pull no science on this shroud, the date will only
lie. She'll tell you it's sacred, even sell you a piece of
the fray. She appears on the cracked ravines of this country
like a ghost on the windshield of an oncoming
train. She refuses to die, but just look at her nation
without a spare penny to change. My wear is a glass made
clean through misuse, the mishandling of my age as revealing
as my erased face, Indian head of my stick birth, my battle
with this neighborhood of avenues scattered with empty shells
of mailboxes, their feet caked with cement like pulled up
pilings? Evidently, they haven't a word

for regret

full heart.

Someday, I said, I can write us both from this mess. But the
key stalls out from under me when I spell your name. I have
to fake the O or go over it again in the dark, a tracing of
differences spilled out on a sheet. If I could stick this
back together, would it stay? It's no rope, I know, and no
good for holding clear liquid. I gather a froth on my gums,
and grin the way an old woman grimaces in a morning mirror.
I was never a clear thing, never felt the way a daughter
feels, never lost out like you, never drove. My moon waits
at the edge of an eagle's aerie, almost extinct and the eggs
are fragile from poisoned ignitions. I'm never coming out of
my cup of tea, never working loose the grease in my hair, the
monkey grease from my dancing elbows that jab at your
shoulder. But I write, and wait for the book to sell, for I
know nothing comes out of it but the past with its widening

teeth, with its meat breath baited at my neck, persistent as the smell of a drunk. Don't tell me. I already know. It's just the rule of the game for the jack of all hearts, and for the queen of baguettes its a cul-de-sac for a joker drawing hearts.

Lucha Corpi

English translations by Catherine Rodríguez-Nieto.

Nineteen

Passion and oracle
logic and secret ritual
tears
sweat and menstrual flow
smiles
the smells of wood and rain-washed narcissus.

Everything not understood by the face
I saw watching me
from across the river
twenty years before the shipwreck.

Mariana

There must be a place in this world
more beautiful
than this merciless city,
happier people perhaps,
over there, beyond the fog.

> But she's chosen to live here
> among the ancient pines

Raised in the neighborhoods of love,
bereft of all her kin:
A husband sacrificed in Korea,
an only son in Vietnam,
two crosses an ocean away,
two medals in a fraying pouch.

> But she's chosen to live here
> among the ancient pines

She's paid her debt
although she never owed a cent.
Even so, her name,
its open vowels
darkened by the sun,
her name is merely
word-play
on the magnetic tape of the wind.

> But she's chosen to live here
> among the ancient pines.

It's Raining

The rains have come
Winter rains
Quiet rains

Oblivious to everything they've come

Falling gray and endless
on the snails
gathered in teeming covens
under the lemon tree,

on the ants
who, exiled from their hills,
carry their dead around
until they drop
under the weight
in a bathtub
or in a cupboard full of bread and honey.

It's raining, it's raining,
Fine rain
Quiet rain
Endless rain . . .

If only a sudden blot of lightning would
cross the sky, swift and bold
            and unannounced,
and the road of thunder shake
            the sclerotic foundations of the city
opposing the dark pulse
            of the wind
            with perfect contrapuntal triads
            light-play
                        noise
                                    silence

But it only goes on raining
Fine rain
Quiet rain
Endless rain

It isn't time, it isn't time . . .

Day's Work

1.
Death is reincarnated in every flower
one city rises on top of another
and in an ordinary street
in the town square
in a gateway
or among flowers and birds
at the edge of the marketplace
two old men look through the garbage
for their daily bread,
a child roams in search of tenderness,
a dark-skinned mother
widowed early of her love
waits in a silent queue
at the factory door.

In an ordinary city
of the old world or of the new
two pair of dark eyes
share one history.

2.

There are nights when the rose hides the thorns
and light goes to find its cause at voice's edge.
These are nights of murmuring, of anxieties repressed,
and though the head on the pillow has forgotten
that tonight the doves flew
buffeted by the wind
and the lilies on the altar fell
riddled with fear,
the spirit toils alone,
even under hardship conditions,
twenty-four hours a day: Our exhausted heart
and weathered kidneys can be transplanted
but our spirit we have always with us
and the tolling bell reminds us at each stroke
that in matters of conscience there are no teachers
and we cannot digest our bread
in someone else's stomach.

3.

Death is reincarnated in every flower . . .

On an ordinary street,
on an ordinary day
time is shot over the sea,
the missile hits its target
with mathematical precision
—and the guerrilla fighter falls,
his vision falling
slowly
on the indifferent cement.

The morning does not restrain
its desire for the day
that's true
but something in us flutters,
plasma floods
into the arteries of the soul,
a new voice takes up residence
in our own
and we realize that we can no longer
like a snake
in the humid heat of August
slough off the fighter's skin
for it has become our own.

Carlos Cumpián

Above Drudgery

for Cynthia

to be Aphrodite today
must be confusing
no one knows a real goddess
when they see one—
no one has the paunch
of patient concern anymore—
flat bellies or nothing.
O archangel of desire
i keep my shirt on while
your apricot mouth
castigates a whole
generation.
your conch shell ears
offer evidence amid
the grimace of
ordinary faces,
your old boyfriend cyclops
reads the paper,
his sunglasses the
size of cymbals.
your damp deity body
lies on a used towel,
while my eyes dehydrate

from following you
like a gladiator
in the desert.

The Survivor: Anishinabe Man

They found a man
who lived in ten
doubled-lined garbage bags
filled with newspapers,
tossed by the downtown crowds,
making a nest for
"no one special,"
just a survivor,
a wastebarrel hunter,
who found the paper that
corporate America hauls
out daily, could cover
his people
across Turtle Island.

He had nine months of rent free
sleeping and eating,
real evidence "the city works,"
even in Christian
chowmein lines,
where "Jesus Saves" and
law 'n' order tools
are sharpened just south
of the Loop.

This soul traveled as
illegal cargo of desire
under the iron horse hulk,
following raw nails until
crippled inside
our hawk-headed town.
He dreamed of Canada
where no exhausted
four wheels made
mad morning rushes
by the big lake.

With no passport,
no marketable wares,
unarmed in the hog's
heart, after winter—
iced eyelids and
dead-moon winds,
you Anishinabe, who's
name I did not catch.
You, pepper-haired warrior,
refused to die, to die
alongside
the once green slant
of the foul expressway,
where your sad
recycled abode
challenged elements and
strange arrows
of motorized millions,
who yesterday
offered small pox blankets

and other offensive coverage
in their reams
of ink-marked sheets.

Coyote Sun

para María Sabina y Anne Waldman

Gathered on Oaxaca's
huarache-worn stones,
made smooth by the soles
of thousands of believers—
never resting on their *petates,*
but dancing the ceremonial *mitote,*
whose inspired beats leaped from a drum
and the mushrooms of language sang
through a poet-priestess—
María Sabina, duality's sister.

We never chanted in a *temaskal,*
never bowed stripped down to a
fire in the sweatlodge as
steam rose from the
lightning bolt's navel
carrying bile and filth to
the bowels of the desert.

You read everything as you listened
to the Folkways record,
and like a bold *sinvergüenza*

you performed *nuestra santa voz*
indígena por los otros.

But, where were the *hongos* of vital skin,
episodes of enrapture with the
living word as prayers passed,
round the candlestar hut.

You missed the children's sweetgrass breath
that prepares the way for hot *aguardiente*
tobacco and food, humble gifts for the ritual
where old man *armadillo* watches
the *Mazatecan* sky, waiting for
his ever-young brother Coyote Sun
to come back up—
Coyote Sun who tricks the
night into chasing him.

María Sabina in a flower *huipil*
adorned with a headdress of
silver braids, aflame with the
medicinal and sacred herbs of Christ.
María Sabina, the one we
talked about so far from
your boulder,
María Sabina, who heard
the jasmine tongue of heaven,
raised her palms to the saints
then clapped and whistled
as the true fast-speaking one,
a *psi*-eyed woman,
the one
who knows Coyote Sun.

Angela de Hoyos

Look Not to Memories

wear your colors
like a present person
       today is
       here & now

let the innocent past
lie
in dignity:
       broken wing
       wilted lily
       shroud

don't look back
the goodbook
advises
       lest you become
       pillar of salt

. . . and I'm a fool
for not discarding
       my worn-out
       bags of guilt

Not Even Because You Have Pearl-White Teeth

delicate blue veins on your legs
a star-mole on your right cheek
and braid your hair
like an Aztek princess

would I consider
Fletcherizing you
into a poem

"poesía no eres tú"
says Rosario Castellanos
and the phrase well-taken
could apply to you

we arachnids
have a reputation
to keep, and if the
genetic lab
catches me asleep, there's
no telling
how they'll re-invent us

. . . uhhhh . . . better go back
to your web
while your limbs
are still intact . . .

pearl-white teeth
are not
my only weakness

Martín Espada

Bully

Boston, Massachusetts, 1987

In the school auditorium,
the Theodore Roosevelt statue
is nostalgic
for the Spanish-American War,
each fist lonely for a saber
or the reins of anguish-eyed horses,
or a podium to clatter with speeches
glorying in the malaria of conquest.

But now the Roosevelt school
is pronounced *Hernández.*
Puerto Rico has invaded Roosevelt
with its army of Spanish-singing children
in the hallways,
brown children devouring
the stockpiles of the cafeteria,
children painting *Taíno* ancestors
that leap naked across murals.

Roosevelt is surrounded
by all the faces
he ever shoved in eugenic spite
and cursed as mongrels, skin of one race,
hair and cheekbones of another.

Once Marines tramped
from the newsreel of his imagination;
now children plot to spray graffiti
in parrot-brilliant colors
across the Victorian mustache
and monocle.

Federico's Ghost

The story is
that whole families of fruitpickers
still crept between the furrows
of the field at dusk,
when for reasons of whiskey or whatever
the cropduster plane sprayed anyway,
floating a pesticide drizzle
over the pickers
who thrashed like dark birds
in a glistening white net,
except for Federico,
a skinny boy who stood apart
in his own green row,
and, knowing the pilot
would not understand in Spanish
that he was the son of a whore,
instead jerked his arm
and thrust an obscene finger.

The pilot understood.
He circled the plane and sprayed again,
watching a fine gauze of poison

drift over the brown bodies
that cowered and scurried on the ground,
and aiming for Federico,
leaving the skin beneath his shirt
wet and blistered,
but still pumping his finger at the sky.

After Federico died,
rumors at the labor camp
told of tomatoes picked and smashed at night,
growers muttering of vandal children
or communists in camp,
first threatening to call Immigration,
then promising every Sunday off
if only the smashing of tomatoes would stop.

Still tomatoes were picked and squashed
in the dark,
and the old women in camp
said it was Federico,
laboring after sundown
to cool the burns on his arms,
flinging tomatoes
at the cropduster
that hummed like a mosquito
lost in his ear,
and kept his soul awake.

Jorge the Church Janitor Finally Quits

Cambridge, Massachusetts, 1989

No one asks
where I am from,
I must be
from the country of janitors,
I have always mopped this floor.
Honduras, you are a squatter's camp
outside the city
of their understanding.

No one can speak
my name,
I host the *fiesta*
of the bathroom,
stirring the toilet
like a punchbowl.
The Spanish music of my name
is lost
when the guests complain
about toilet paper.

What they say
must be true:
I am smart,
but I have a bad attitude.

No one knows
that I quit tonight,
maybe the mop

will push on without me,
sniffing along the floor
like a crazy squid
with stringy gray tentacles.
They will call it Jorge.

Niggerlips

Niggerlips was the high school name
for me.
So called by Douglas
the car mechanic, with green tattoos
on each forearm,
and the choir of round pink faces
that grinned deliciously
from the back row of classrooms,
droned over by teachers
checking attendance too slowly.

Douglas would brag
about cruising his car
near sidewalks of black children
to point an unloaded gun,
to scare niggers
like crows off a tree,
he'd say.

My great-grandfather Luis
was un *negrito* too,
a shoemaker in the coffee hills
of Puerto Rico, 1900.

The family called him a secret
and kept no photograph.
My father remembers
the childhood white powder
that failed to bleach
his stubborn copper skin,
and the family says
he is still a fly in milk.

So Niggerlips has the mouth
of his great-grandfather,
the song he must have sung
as he pounded the leather and nails,
the heat that courses through copper,
the stubbornness of a fly in milk,
and all you have, Douglas,
is that unloaded gun.

Two Mexicanos Lynched in Santa Cruz, California, May 3, 1877

More than the moment
when forty gringo vigilantes
cheered the rope
that snapped two Mexicanos
into the grimacing sleep of broken necks,

more than the floating corpses,
trussed like cousins of the slaughterhouse,
dangling in the bowed mute humility
of the condemned,

more than the *Virgen de Guadalupe*
who blesses the brownskinned
and the crucified,
or the guitar-plucking skeletons
they will become
on the *Día de los Muertos,*

remain the faces of the lynching party:
faded as pennies from 1877, a few stunned
in the blur of execution,
a high-collar boy smirking, some peering
from the shade of bowler hats, but all
crowding into the photograph.

La Tumba de Buenaventura Roig

for my great-grandfather, died 1941

Buenaventura Roig,
once peasants in the thousands
streamed down hillsides
to witness the great eclipse
of your funeral.
Now your bones have drifted
with the tide of steep grass,
sunken in the chaos of weeds
bent and suffering
like canecutters in the sun.
The drunken caretaker
cannot find the grave,
squinting at your name,

spitting as he stumbles
between the white Christs
with hands raised
sowing their field
of white crosses.

Buenaventura Roig,
in Utuado you built the stone bridge
crushed years later by a river
raving like a forgotten god;
here sweat streaked your face
with the soil of coffee,
the ground where your nephew slept
while rain ruined the family crop,
and his blood flowered like flamboyán
on the white suit of his suicide.

Buenaventura Roig,
in the town plaza where you were mayor,
where there once was a bench
with the family name,
you shouted subversion
against occupation armies and sugarcane-patrones
to the jíbaros who swayed
in their bristling dry thicket of straw hats,
who knew bundles and sacks
loaded on the fly-bitten beast
of a man's back.

Buenaventura Roig,
not enough money for a white Christ,
lost now even to the oldest gravedigger,
the one with an English name

descended from the pirates of the coast,
who grabs for a shirt-pocket cigarette
as he remembers your funeral,
a caravan trailing in the distance
of the many years
that cracked the skin around his eyes.

Buenaventura Roig,
we are small among mountains,
and we listen for your voice
in the peasant chorus of five centuries,
waiting for the cloudburst of wild sacred song,
pouring over the crypt-wreckage of graveyard,
over the plaza and the church
where the statue of San Miguel
still chokes the devil with a chain.

Alicia Gaspar de Alba

Elemental Journey: Anniversary Gift

1.
Adirondack Park

When the map blossomed green
in upstate New York, halfway to Canada,
we said, *let's camp here!*
And followed route 28 north
into this huge green organ,
this wild heart
of New England heavy
with lakes and pines,
bear, coon, crow, deer.
Who could have imagined our future
would contain such wilderness?

Three years ago, we spread
my grandmother's crocheted blanket
on Revere Beach. We wore white
woven Mexican dresses, Navajo beads,
huaraches. We lit candles,
slipped silver bands
on each other's fingers, spoke
our intentions so simply
we no longer remember what we said.
To crown the ceremony
Liliana cast white crysanthemums,
I gave cornflowers
to the Atlantic, asking the Mother

to bless this joining
of *corazón, alma y cuerpo.*

Today, we awaken to raindrops on the tent,
soaked spruce and wood smoke.
We go for breakfast in town, Inlet
of the forest, amazed at how the hills
swell with mist, float in the distance
like dreams.

Last night, watching the orange print
of the fire, I worried life was too much
of a miracle and Liliana said:
We've learned how to make decisions.
It's deciding that's so difficult,
that makes life seem an enemy.

Oh, life, Oh Mother Planet, you are not the enemy!

From your iron core you speak to us
in your tongue of hurricanes
and droughts. Tornadoes whirl
your message, your great sorrow
quakes under our feet.

In a dream I watched blue
fallout sifting through the earth,
pink particles of a strange light
dropping on the bodies of children,
their mouths oozing mercury
like spoiled fish.

Here in the woods, on this
journey toward waterfalls
I can hear your green heart
and feel blessed, pretend the whole
universe is a child swimming.

2.
Swimming in Limekiln Lake

I dived to heal
my lungs, shake
the congestion loose,
uncoil my spine
in the cold water.
Nipples rubbing
on the shallows,
I remembered how
as a girl I played Tarzan
and learned to hold my breath long enough
to dance with crocodiles,
save Jane
from the water monsters,
the jungle ghosts.

I dived to be inside
the Mother's belly,
the end of my thirtieth year
looming like a thunderhead.
Once I was afraid to die
at thirty. I know how
each birthday is a death.

The reeds growing in the lake
slough off my used skin, the past
rises from the water like steam.
Liliana is napping on the beach.
She cannot join me in this
ritual of rebirth.

3.
Waking Up in Ontario: Reward

Because we were lost, because
we had not reached the Canadian woods

and had to pitch camp on the lawn
of Knight's Hideaway Park,

we turned our tent
to face the trees, our back

window to the row of trailers
rooted in the electric lots.

Our lot dark as the Adirondacks
though we heard no branches

breaking three feet from the tent,
no black bears,

no deer or raccoon sniffing
at our Birkenstocks.

We slept like tired girls,
hardly moving, our dreams

weighing down the night.
The darkness, the moist grass, the stars

swarming silver through the oaks
marked the trail to the Mother's womb.

Nothing in our dreams predicted
that sunrise convergence of song,

how the trees blazed with warbler,
robin, blue jay, redwing blackbird,

sparrow, crow—their voices bursting
like fireworks out of the leaves.

4.
The Niagara River Speaks Three Languages

Upriver

Up here, there's no hurry.
Willows tilt along the bank
and creeks spill like childhood
memories into the flow: the time
Grandpa bought me a dwarf-sized shovel
to help him plant rosebushes in the backyard;
the time I rode a bus to Disneyland,
nine years old, no family, the tour-
guide my father's girlfriend; the time
I came home from school and found
our dog Sanson stiff under an army blanket.

The paved road by the water
is hardly used. All the attention

is nine miles downriver
where the Falls fill cameras
and absorb the energy of every tourist.
If you dont' believe me,
notice, the next time you ride
the Maid of the Mist, how your heart
rattles as you cross the rainbow, almost
at the foot of the Falls, how your lungs
heave and nearly break open in the wild
splashing and churning of the water.
Notice how exhausted you are
after humbling yourself
to that part of the river.

Up here, there are no expectations.
Every creek and bridge you pass,
every picnic table and docked boat,
every tent and window breathes
of solitude. You can build
up your strength on this quiet
Canadian road.

The Falls

You see, even if I am boycotted
by the grandmother who pressed warm
flannel cloths to my chest when cough
stormed my lungs, and even if
the uncles who tossed me in the air
and took me to the movies
and gave me quarters for *domingo* turn
their shoulderblades to my lesbian
life, I will keep thundering

through the course I have chosen
to carve for myself. True,
the falling, roaring tumult of water
separates two countries.
This border is wider and more dangerous
than the Río Grande, but the bridge
balanced over the gorge is called
Rainbow Bridge. The iris
is another infinite lesson.

Whirlpool Rapids

It used to be popular to tempt
the rapids. Men and women in barrels,
on tightropes, hoping their names
would be forever linked to Niagara.
Such a whirl of human folly
this thirst for fame, this need to compete
with the Mother's power. Today,
in a small room two-hundred-thirty feet
into the gorge, the daredevils' names
and pictures decorate the walls.
You forget them as soon as the rapids
crash into view, or you shake
your head at their courage, their choice
of a shortcut to the Otherworld.
Of course, not all of them died.
Some were found tumbling in the whirlpool,
deaf and dizzy, but more defiant
than the water breaking on the rocks.

Through the canyon of my life,
defiance is a vein of flowing crystal,
fed by rain and tempered
on ninety-degree turns.

5.
Rainstorm: The Gorge

The suddenness,
like everything else,
is a gift,
a way the Mother has
of inviting you to listen
longer, learn the three
languages of the river.

At Boyer's Creek the river spoke
a whispered, ancient tongue
that lapped at the stones
of your memory.
At Horseshoe Falls you trembled,
the wild mares of the moon
galloping into your bones.

Here, the rapids roil with lust,
churning like the wet
dream of a giant woman
in whose depths the gorge
is but a ligament
to an even deeper
and more electrifying
storm.

6.
Piseco Lake

Back at Adirondack Park
I watch a blond boy
smoothing a space on the beach
for the sandcastle
that will moat his loneliness.
Other boys shout *Marco!*
Polo! in the water
and three girls chase
after attention in their tight suits.
The castle builder dips
his pail into the lake,
mixes the water with sand
to shape his walls and towers.
I wonder if he remembers
the Mother's song or the cave
walls he painted with buffalo blood
in another life.
I wonder if he will grow
into a man who cleaves
to another man,
to poetry or photography,
if he will choose
not to attend his father's funeral,
if he will take an elemental journey
like this one
and find himself
on the edge of water
inhaling time
as quiet

and luminous
as the heart of quartz.

7.
Point Comfort: Coming Home

Humpbacks in the clouds
hedge this amethyst twilight.
The lake surrenders
its clarity, swallows
the misty secrets of the trees.
Potatoes roast on the fire
as I slice onions, watching you
shoulder camera and tripod
to Lake Pisecos shore—
the negatives
of all the water
you have shot swirling
in the dark room
of your memory.
The light you cannot dodge
or burn will blaze from the bones
of these images.

It would be so easy to return
to the earth without a purpose
or a coffin. Life is enough
to humble anyone.

The evening grows its black fur.
I toss greens, transfixed
by this love affair
with the woods,

this birth of silence
over the water.

You and I will leave
the North heavy
with joy,
black bears fishing
in our blood.

Rebecca Gonzales

Flesh and Blood

1.
Dear Mother,
The day before the baby was born,

I dreamed I was pure as Eve,
lying in a bower of white roses,
under the reaching sun of the Garden

when the baby spurted out cleanly
between my legs
without a cry.

I thought you'd understand
if I told you that when I woke,
I'd never been so afraid.

2.
I spent hours at work
processing words into columns of print
used to build pages of news

while you piece hollow lengths of pipe
into scaffolds for boilermakers climbing
storage tanks at the refinery.

And as tomorrow's pages are laid out,
and the night shift dismantles your work,
we come home

with only our blood to warm us.

3.
Even though I was a girl
father expected me to be brave

as he held down
a soft *cabrito* and slit its throat.

Its eyes trolled in pools of white;
its cries lagged in the quickness of blood.

"It's just blood," my father would say.
"It didn't keep him alive,

and though it'll feed us,
it won't keep us alive either."

4.
A bull can be chuted
into a bullfighting arena
and waste no time
figuring what it's all about.

Let the cocky matador walk off,
spicing his steps with art,
he'll stake his territory and stay,
pawing the sand.

Let the crowd see visions of truth
in this blazing heat,
he'll hold the world
between his horns till then.

Let the blood foam on his back;
it's only blood.
If it brings him to his knees,
he'll spit at the thought
of shade and a quiet pasture.

Reading the Sky

The morning is quiet with unanswered questions;
I read the sky from the back-door porch,
feeling secrets spiral around me,
tease from tunnels of sunlight going deep in the woods.

My coffee cup holds it all in dark shimmer;
I drink, filling with answers
when a rooster's crow startles me.
I make too much of things.

Out on the lake,
birds pick fish
out of the sun, think nothing of it;
they know where they are.

Mornings we can survive;
light is warmth;
shade, our refuge,
but nights don't read the same way.

We can moon over an elusive night all we want;
we hold nothing but flesh.
So let's open the windows,
leave the lights on tonight;

let's lie naked in an empty house;
let the moon fight the clouds
to stare at us,
figure out what we mean.

Superstition

The tree moth in the garage was an omen,
so I killed the messenger:
pulled off its velvet wings
and chewed them with a spiteful mouth.

A delicate crunch of the veins
and I heard nothing else.
My tongue grew thick with their moss.
I swallowed its wisdom with a vengeful mouth
and tasted my own fear.

To the Newlyweds in the Barrio

Subtract the size of the world
from an empty stomach
and over the difference construct a roof.

Wall up hunger,
give it no room to spread
to the eyes, hands and feet.

Later you'll be able to afford a TV
to bring you reports
of soldiers invading with their shadows.

But for the time
all you can afford is a radio
and guilt as you dance around in your house.

Ray González

The Sustenance

"I inhabit a sacred wound.
I inhabit imaginary ancestors."
— AIMÉ CÉSAIRE

Campesinos bend in the 115 degree heat,
dig the holes of history,
disappear without a trace
when the family comes north to build
the great desert railroads.
My grandparents, *Julia y Bonifacio,*
married at fourteen to escape
la revolución for Arizona railroad camps,
where Yaquis laid the tracks,
special teams walking ahead of the line
to clean the Sonora desert
of great, five-foot rattlesnakes,
dozens of them slowing the railroad,
taking out a worker, here and there,
defying the cuts in the earth,
workers killing and bagging them,
living on snake meat
to get across the desert.

Bonifacio, the foreman, often refused
snake meat, packing beans and tortillas
Julia made at three every morning.
Once, he had to bite into the fried meat,
fresh out of the campfire.

He burned his mouth.
"*Cabrón! Chingao!*"
He threw the meat into the dirt,
the silent workers staring at him,
wondering if he knew it was
bad luck to waste what
the desert gave to them.

That tossed meat dried into
a greasy spot in the sand,
attracted flies and ants,
even the buzzard hovering
after the tracks had grown
another ten miles,
the rattlers crawling out
as the sun went down,
thick giants overlooked
in the path of progress,
unaware the spoiled slice of meat
would be washed away by the rains
that fell and fell,
flooded everything
that unforgettable year,
three days after my grandfather died
of a heart attack, Christmas, 1941.

Rattlesnake Dance, Coronado Hills, El Paso, 1966

after the photo "Hopi Snake Dance" by Edward Curtis

1.
Snakes in the mouth.
From the ground to the mouth, to the sky,
dancers curl in a circle to gather
snakes, carry them in their mouths,
dance for rain, their faces painted
like blind snakes of the firstborn,
snakes that cannot see, but sense
where the heart beats,
where to strike after the dance,
after the rain.

2.
I climb up the steep arroyo,
listen for the rattle,
a boy of fourteen in search of
the rattler I spotted the day before,
its quickness behind rocks
the stillness of dirt walls,
a sign there is nothing
to hang onto,
until I trip and fall,
roll a few yards down, laughing,
calling to my friends to climb up,
not knowing they ran when they heard it,
not knowing I had climbed too far.

3.
Women and children watch the dance
from the high walls.
Only the men gather the snakes
in their mouths,
only the men can pick them up,
wear them like new arms and legs
coming rapidly alive, appendages
crawling into the body to make it whole.

4.
I found it nailed to the wooden fence,
the rattle cut off,
its skin peeled back,
left hanging in the breeze,
stiff patterns blowing like paper
with an alphabet burned in blood,
the killer leaving the skin
as a god exposing the fate of snakes
to those who follow them,
beauty of the large, flat head
crushed into the wood,
its pure instinct beaten back
before it kissed the follower,
branded him with the fire that
must, someday, enter the body,
wash it of desire and breath,
swell it to the size of dying,
shape it into the form
this one will never take,
as I pull it off the fence,
watch it twist and dissolve
into the ground.

5.
One dancer bends over,
grabs two rattlers in one hand,
his grace in the sun
a stain in the photo,
his disappearance in the circle
a sign two snakes coiled
into the bone of song,
muscles given and granted
like flutes of rain
that fall around
the tightening chests
of the exhausted men.

6.
After killing three of them,
I saw the fourth climb up the porch,
squeeze into the bricks, disappear
into a corner of the house,
its body vanishing into the wall,
becoming a part of our home.
I never saw it, again,
but lay awake at night,
knowing it was inside the house,
trapped between wood and mortar,
moving from room to room without rattling,
waiting for the walls to crumble,
waiting for the boy to press his hands
against the wall above the bed,
push in the dark, tap and push,
the silence of a falling, black wall
that smothered every breath
I took as I waited and waited.

7.
The dancers run and chant,
faster and faster,
dozens of snakes crossing their feet,
more falling off painted bodies,
blending into hair and masks,
clinging to necks
so the dancers can hold
and embrace each other.
The circle grows smaller and smaller,
snakes flying through legs,
women and children staring from above,
the pit of dancers growing deeper
with the drums and rattles,
the round floor of the earth
suddenly collapsing under them,
opening to let men and snakes
go their way,
choose to hide or reveal
how much blood to let per beat,
how much blood, per rattle,
to spit into the starting rain.

Snakeskin   (*A Dream*)

I thought the rattlesnake was dead
and I stuck my finger in its mouth,
felt the fangs bite down,
penetrate me
without letting go,
the fire removing my eyes,

replacing them with
green light of the reptile
that illuminated my hand.

It entered my bone and blood,
until my whole arm was green and damp,
my whole left side turning
slick and cool as
I tried to pull it
out of my body.

I peeled my skin back
to find my veins were green
and held tightly what I believed,
what forced itself into me,
what I allowed to be given
without knowing

I would carry that secret,
crawl over the ground,
become a fusion of muscle
only the sun steps on.
I leaned against a huge boulder,
sweated, waited, slept,
and, by morning, found a new way
of embracing that rock,
new life in the green flesh
of the world.

Three Snakes, Strawberry Canyon, Berkeley

The Rattlesnake

We really didn't see it,
but the guy walking ahead of us
said it struck and missed him.
He pointed to the tall grass.
"If you get closer,
you can see its eyes."
We looked, but couldn't see it
and kept walking.
I thought about the rattlers
I killed as a boy,
back home in Texas,
the nest of six baby rattlers
we found in the yard,
my mother insisting I cut
their heads off with a shovel,
saying the babies were more lethal
because they could fill you with venom,
and not know when to pull back
like adult snakes.
I recalled how I killed them
and regret it still,
and wanted this rattler
to bite the hiker so I could forget
his bravery, his wonder.

The Garter Snake

It looked like an overgrown worm,
tiny and quick as it flashed

across the trail,
its sidewinding motion
leaving marks in the dirt.
As we noticed it, we forgot
what we said about poetry,
how those things vanish,
then reappear before us,
how we admit black and green bands
of the garter snake
are the same colors
we keep missing each time
we try to write anything.

The Gopher Snake

We found it sleeping
in the middle of the trail.
It didn't move,
but glistened as we approached,
but I knew it wasn't the rattler
that haunts my footsteps.
This snake looked
like a giant slug,
a slow, wet creature
that sunned itself
so it could dissolve
into the ground.
Suddenly, we realized
it was good luck
to have snakes cross our path
like the unknown pulses

in the earth that
traveled underground,
ahead of us, all the way
to the bottom of
the surprising, moving canyon.

Víctor Hernández Cruz

Two Guitars

Two guitars were left in a room all alone
They sat on different corners of the parlor
In this solitude they started talking to each other
My strings are tight and full of tears
The man who plays me has no heart
I have seen it leave out of his mouth
I have seen it melt out of his eyes
It dives into the pores of the earth
When they squeeze me tight I bring
Down the angels who live off the chorus
The trios singing loosen organs
With melodious screwdrivers
Sentiment comes off the hinges
Because a song is a mountain put into
Words and landscape is the feeling that
Enters something so big in the harmony
We are always in danger of blowing up
With passion
The other guitar:
In 1944 New York
When the Trío Los Panchos started
With Mexican & Puerto Rican birds
I am the one that one of them held
Tight like a woman
Their throat gardenia gardens
An airport for dreams
I've been in theatres in cabarets

I played in an apartment on 102nd street
After a baptism pregnant with women
The men flirted and were offered
Chicken soup
Echoes came out of hallways as if from caves
Someone is opening the door now
The two guitars hushed and there was a
Resonance in the air like what is left by
The last chord of a *bolero*

Don Arturo Says:

When I was young
there was no difference
Between the way I danced
and the way tomatoes
Converted themselves
Into sauce
I did the waltz or a
guaguancó
Which every one your rhythm
which every one your song
The whole town was caressed
to sleep with my two-tone
Shoes
Everyone
had to leave me alone
On the dirt or on the wood
they used to come from afar

and near
Just to say look at Arturo
disappear.

Geography of the Trinity Corona

Galicia Gypsy tongue sucks salt water
Red fish *gitana* de Galicia
Sings
Romany *de* Hindus
Romany *de* Hindus
Ibéricos boats from the soul
Boats from Ibéricos lust
Schizophrenic ships search golden dust
Ladinos
Ladinos
Ancient Spanish
Ancient Spanish
Lengua del Kábala
Kábala *lengua*
O Mohamet flor *del este*
Flor este del Mohamet
Sonrisa of same people
Flor de maya
Lengua primordial agua y sal
Mora eyes of paradise
Gypsy Freeway
Gypsy Freeway
Mohamet
Ladinos
Romany *de* Hindus

Valencia
Where sound parked in the tongue
Galicia *con pan*
Pan Galicia
Pan pan Ibéricos
Bridge made of white handkerchiefs
To the cascabells of Andalusia
Walking light on the loose
Gone through the strings of sitars
Guitars / Sitars
My strings are here
A sí
Cádiz *cámara* my friends
In the pupils of time
Jump barefoot into the circle dance
Here come the Romanies
Islamicals
The Rock of Gibraltar
Rock of Tarik
Like the wave of the ocean
After retreat

On the sand it leaves pearls
From the bottom
Shaped like three-dimensional mandalas

Take my boat
Take my boat

Gallegos *gitanos*
Jump the Arawaks
The *michicas*
Who had gold like we have the air

Golden halos
Of Maya Cocos
Tainos skidding through
Carib sea on canoes
Church pierced the mountain
Gallelocos everywhere
Cement came down from heaven
Taíno areyto echoes from the flora
Gone through the pipe of time
Into the face
Into the cheek so cute
España danza
Africoco bembé
Burundanga mixture is the word
Bembe Mohamet *Areyto*
Layered peacock cake
Sandwhich of language

Take my boat
Take my boat

Yoruba y Arare
Lucumi
Cascabels of Romany gypsies
Nativo antillano
Hindus
Gallegos
Africano
Caribe
Rythmic circle
The islands are beads
of a necklance
Tarot cards with tobacco smoke

Crescent moon
The handshake of Fatima
Golden and red hot rubies
Chains where sacraments hang
Symphony of
Moorish flamenco
Fans opening like sound
Out of the acoustic mama bass
Streets of Islam wrapped in
Catholic robes
Where they say an eye for an eye
Teeth for teeth
Jump for jump
Make my Spanish lamp
Make my Spanish lamp
Walk the camels into the gardens
Electric flowers
See them shine
Make my Indian time
Make my Indian time
Song is memory
Memory is song
Take my boat
Take my boat
Make my African Alphabet
Skin on skin

Mohamet Africanos
Look the street is full of
Ethiopians
Look Jersey City full of
Taínos
Gitanos lindos

Lucumi inside Yucaye
White angels come from
Arare drums
Visual spectacle envied
by rainbow
Look Pakistani mambo
The ears are the musical race
Even polish my Polish
Mazurka in the *guava* villages
Blood vessels of combined chemistry
From everywhere to someone
Galicia
Romany *de* Hindus
Arawaki
Arare
Moro
Lucumi
Iberios
Mohammedans
Gypsy
Yoruba
Taínos
Colors turn into sounds
We start building cities
From blueprints
Found in the sails
Of remember

Take my boat
Take my boat

Invisibility 0

Planets of air
angels and music
between us all
Humidity penetrated
by a screw of molecules
Global bubbles
pink and hazy
Glass teeth without
bodies
invisible gobs of manure
synchronized with space
Waves
Transparent porky-dogs
Monsters created by
anteaters fucking mountain
Swine in thought
A worm the size of
a ship moving
Between the cities
Dressed in ultraviolet fog
Insane moans moving
thru hallway of clouds
Where fly holy spirit birds
who eat electric umbilical
wires
Which are plugged into the
hole in your soul
Melting into vagabundo spirits
vacationing in matter
Chunks of atmosphere

between us
Folks is full of monstrous
images
which make horror flicks seem
polite
Earth contaminated
by objects of unknown dimensions

With breaths of sulfuric gasses
Passages of murky soup
like hippopotamus saliva
Mixed with bull's brain
and school yard basketball
Players sweat
Mist of carbon dioxide
on wings of bats with
Vampires lust
The discussion minerals are
having made visible in three
Dimensions
Lead transmitting rays to copper
Copper smoking into silver
Silver music begging the ears
of gold
Talking about alchemy
The man who ate a dollar bill
and shitted four quarters
Sheet of memory traveling
endless planks of atoms
Juices of emotion making
lightning sounds from Mars
Luciferian radiation beaming
down from Venus

Primeval spaces where tobacco
was a theory
A telephone call from Caquax
Mountains whose dress is a
gown of blue crystals called sky
Orchestra of reptilian musicians
blowing into caves like trumpets
Echoes make the heavens
shingaling
Ears floating without flesh
like helium balloons
Fall into dance position
Making an oval like the
island of Puerto Rico
Moose and bull horns
are antennas for cable
Thoughts of red fragrance
Dreams of Andalusian pirates
masturbating into Atlantic Ocean
After seeing Cordova mermaids
pop out the water in their heads
Vengeful skeletons jumping out
of air pockets
Collecting cemetery prayers
and candle fumes
Between us is doors made of the
aroma of dead flowers
Azucenas and *condiamores*
the campana of hallucinogenic flight
a firm of words which are pictures
over the Florida trees red sparks
Shooting from Jagueyes barrio
in mountain so high

Nectar left by butterflies
in their tranquil flight
Bees hear bells blasting
out of black coffee cups and orbit
like sputniks around the earth
the sky looks like a page
full of clouds
above the cross of the Catholic
church

Over Aguas Buenas the Virgin of
Monserrate jumps rope from stars
to moon
With her blue cape
She empties out into the irises
of sleeping girls
Who wake up open their windows
and with their moorish eyes
Put the flowers to sleep

Between us is a lake of humidity
Where sound is like light bulbs
Space cadets shift into memory
Memory makes a horn of air
Where your desires sparkle
and beg eternity for love.

Juan Felipe Herrera

The Boy of Seventeen

The boy of seventeen
twists in the sheets
the pages of sex
        the bolts are crying
        the windows are crying
his legs sweat camphor
and his blue lips
are dissolved into his cheeks
the pillows' hollows
are withering
        the door is crying
        seeing the keys
        the clock cries
        burning the curtains
the boy of seventeen
a paragraph of rain
between silk and marble
he measures the nails
in Christ's arms
he wants an X
on the left side of his dreams

        he's searching for his mother
        naked on the red altar

Water Girl

for Almasol

Girl of water
and lips of fruit
the windows hold a grudge
and the asphalt is choking under an old car

girl of water
and guitars of violets
the walls are in mourning
last night the old roof died
thinking of the sea and the clear breeze

girl of water
and saffron of march
the happy grass kneeled down
the wind broke one of its arms
in a theater of reeds
embracing a thorn

girl of water
because the sun is a farm of tied-up irises
because crying is an arrow of green hands
because they bound the dove with seven nails in may
because men whip themselves in a banquet of chains

girl of water
with the rain between your teeth
and blue boats in your words

what are you looking at in this long deep night?

Earth Chorus

for the campesinos of Las Cabañas, a municipality of El Salvador
and for Philippe Bourgeois

It is the earth that snarls and slashes with black jaguar
eyes and teeth and incandescent claws
the Pharoah
and his troops of delicate overcoat and medal delight
it is the earth that reveals lies and recognizes with
lightning and birds and bare feet and adolescent brows
and cheekbones of lava
the traitor
and his wire hands and plantation laws and slave labor
it is the earth flowing the dew of brave women
and men on march with rivers and coffee plantations with salt
and fury
it is the earth that determines the new furrows the knives
of plants of shining flesh the skin rising
the viper of rhymes and guerrilla war breathing fire
extinguishing the plague the silk web the false tower
it is the earth
that hurls red whips and elastic bodies
infinite fingers and invisible legs that fly and smash
the final throne the miniscule lie the throat and
fist of the general the boss the shocked supervisor
it is the earth with its moss and its deep ovaries and sperm
that spill their honey and sweat and unleash the rain and
purify with their heat
it is the earth
that recognizes the squadron of planes the uniform of shadows
and silver

Words
Paper.

I am working on a play—the world in twenty years.
There is a sentry, a clown and warrior; a slave colony
on the verge of escape from the video eye. The eye
sees everything. Picture the slender man in the supermarket
holding up a small can of cranberry sauce—weighing
the contents he is concerned with a stamp-size
inscription. Ingredients:

sodium fructose,
pectin, artificial flavoring.

Tomorrow his daughter will bleed from the mouth;
the blood will glisten hot, wavy—her tall boyfriend drinks.
She runs to him; he traps her when daddy sleeps.

There are too many recorded tragedies. No one listens.
Listen to the little bronze gears inside the computer;
everyone owns one, delivers upon the keys. Listen again:

the A
the Z
the Asterisk
slapping, so quiet,
mournful, so pious.

Treacheries.
Falsehoods.

Big words. My friends are afraid to speak them.
The television offers brilliant young men,

immense shoulder braces tumbling across the green,
a pigskin against the solar plexus, a broken leg
juts out wanting to kick the audience, sweltering,
saliva on shirts, ribbons, cold bottle Pepsi's.
I work towards good things, play inexpensive games—
a miniature clay house with two black windows,
pearled marbles with yellowish zig-zag lines,
a funny thumb-size, plastic, German lugar pistol.
I surprise myself. I finally figured people out.

The Rhyme-Master, Elder King of Ink
who bequethes Grace upon the Speechless.

The Child-Molester who receives tribute
from his political colleagues.

The Daughter-Monkey caged by her own aging mother
who will never talk to another man again.

I think of my mother. Tiny ancient—who saved broken birds
from the sidewalk rubbing their heads with herbs who
waited nineteen years for me to return. I never did.
I read about the Thalamus, the intricate web of the brain.
My friends use these words too:

Literary Production
Feminist Art
Ideology—the Underclass

while our little mothers shrink,
die without us. We never say Sacrifice. It smells of
religion.
My Aunt Lela is caught in a second-story above a ham and eggs

diner. She's eight-four when she walks she falls
on the cement every time her legs give out.
I tell her use a cane like my mother did.

People don't like to hear this, they say poetry must have
a fancy curl in the center—don't complain, they say.
I ask them do you have better figures?

In the United States
the per capita income is $27,000 a year
in Malawi Africa its $160 in Nayarit Mexico up
on Indian land—a bowl of corn squash and seeds.

I sit at the library, gaze across the table; trees, windows
are continuous; the telephone post connects with the leaves
darkness crawls up the bark, tears daylight to pieces.
These are labels and empty synonyms:

Poetry and chalkdust.
Horror and humanity.
Laughter and spit.

I tell my son—that's good, learn the cello, listen to
its womb, take your time, observe, survive.

Pyramid of Supplications

I just read the headlines.

First Tremor's Toll Reaches
2000 confirmed dead—Sept. 21, 1985

Everytime I walk Mexico City
I smell petroleum. It's so sweet.
I change into someone else.

I am a swanky Chicano bopping down San Juan de Letrán
talking about *La Colonia del Niño Perdido* where
my mother's from or I am rapping about the next train
to Veracruz or

I am just heading towards *La Torre Metropolitana*
to make a deal with the literary honchos.

How about a special supplement on New Raza poetry
from California, the Southwest?
(Who would travel so far to get published?)

I am from here.
A stranger that never left.

The streets
are always lined with hands,
small ones, begging.

Now, her hands, his hands are underground;
still asking, tangled in a crevice, falling, still expecting,
groping for her father's chair, descending,
still reaching for the warmth of a cardboard shield,
tumbling under the final tear of their miniature candle,
he screams for his lover's shawl, his daughter's memory
slipping further into the arms of his anonymous war.

I can hear the rosaries beneath the quivering backs
still turning over her fingers, still waiting
for his salvation,

still darkening.

Perhaps, foodstuffs will be distributed to the living.
Who knows?

Undoubtedly,
the presidents will talk about reconstruction
and the tourists will travel without fear (again).

Will we be here still falling?
Who will write about it?

I have never wanted to surrender,
not even to death's sudden ripening glow.

But, here, in this final burial,
there are no real choices.

The blue baby and the dignitary with a brief mustache,
a young Mexican Adelia studying to be an agronomist,
Chico, the shoe-shine-kid and the PSUM revolutionary
are still alive, all alive

in this dark carousel
of no mercy and no forgiveness.

Rita Magdaleno

On the Way to the Reunion

1.

On the way to the reunion in copper country,
Highway 77 heading into Globe, I pass
Dripping Springs Wash and Winkleman, a black
scarf looped around my neck, gold threads
running through it. Across the Gila River,
someone is reading the Sunday paper.
In Valentine Park, a scatter
of little trailers huddle together,
silent. And one small bar.

2.

At the reunion in Ice Box Canyon,
they're having a dance on the patio.
Menudo y Bloody Marys, *cilantro* chopped
coarsely. Cold Sunday morning,
music provided by the Corvettes,
a woman singing clearly, "Hold on
. . . we won't let you down."

3.

At the Serbian Cemetery, a massive yucca
stretches over one segregated plot, the grave
of "Sambo," who was baptized *Mino Cano,*
a boxer who walked around dead drunk
and severely bowlegged. Little man
who came to my father's wedding reception

on the porch in Grover Canyon, 1944.
Sambo had threatened to shoot Otello,
Lucy y Teddy's dog. Sambo, he came
to my father's small white wedding.

4.
In Grover Canyon, I'm looking for the house
where my father grew up. It's gone. Still,
I have the memory of trees, two Alamo
out front and a desert Holly Berry
by the back door. My tía told me about the trees
and my grandfather. He died at 42, Ash Wednesday,
and his friend who drove the rail cars
at Inspiration Mine still blames himself
for my grandfather's death. He still lives
in the canyon, sends apologetic notes to my Nana.
She is losing her memory and I'm driving past
Pinto Lane, three black mine cars straddling
the top of a white hill above Claypool.
On this road out of Grover Canyon,
two dogs run wild and a man is coming
out of the Lariat Lounge, brown
Sunday afternoon.

5.
At the Copper Creek gift shop, my tía buys
wild honey and a pair of peridot earrings.
A large collection of knives glisten
under glass. A Brazilian agate
is the only gift I buy myself.
In the coffee shop next door,
some lonesome cowboy music wails,
"I ain't gonna live forever . . ."

6.
On the way home at sunset, I stop
at El Capitán Pass. Kit Carson tried
to forge a way through here
and described it as impassable.
Dusk, watercolors of light, pink
and lavendar are running into the canyon.
Also, a blue deep as the bowels
and sun tumbling slowly now
into one misty gorge. Behind me,
a trail of headlights loops down
Highway 77. South, like a delicate
chain of old pearls,
a clear way home.

Rosary

Crystal beads slide
from her hands falling
forward and around
and round
      the silver
cross dangles
a small Christ
      each
Sunday on St. Anthony's
hardwood pews
her fingers count
beads and fumble
through a strand
of decades to repeat

the mysteries and
         again
recall the lush green
of Aguascalientes
where she bore
my father at sixteen
then rode the migrant
train to a mining town
where she dried
meat on a tin roof
for years
for children
         then wrapped
the last one
Pepita's twin
in a shoe box and
buried my grandfather
         in 1943
when he broke
inside a black pocket
of the Inspiration Mine
         each
Sunday the same
ritual of prayers.

Fall Reunion

for my grandfather, Andrés

In Grover Canyon,
oak leaves curl gold
and the stripped hills
are brown, *café
con leche*, children
playing tug of war
on a dirt road.
Earlier, your daughters
laced pink silk roses
over you, a century
plant breathing high
above the weeds
and candles, a simple
crucific, plots
and headstones, wild
desert, a small piece
of malachite blue
on the gravel road
stretching to you. This
simple life: to get up
at dawn, to make
the long drive here
where I will begin
to pose among the dead,
rearrange myself
on top of you. This
intimacy of fathers
and daughters, history

shaped from the center
of the soul. Late
rain breathing
all around us.

On Maricopa Road

for Nana

Her house is wide open, a shack house
with no inside doors.
Just a pale yellow curtain
drawn across the doorway
between the kitchen and bedroom
of Mary y Pepita, mis tías.
And the house more like a box
real hot in June.

When I was seven I lived there
and I could see
the kitchen sink if I stood
real hard on my toes
on the tip of the bed. Then,
I leaned into the small window
in the wall that divided up
the bedroom from the old blue
kitchen. Good smells.
Cilantro, garlic, and onion
sliced thin and sweet.

Funny how the curtain,
real old and thin, kept
things divided up. Even though
privacy was never a big deal
and there was always room
for me in the bed
between mis tías. Each morning,
I walked to St. Anthony's church
to get ready for my First Communion.
We learned how to sing,
"Come, Oh Holy Spirit,"
and I learned how to tell
half-truths in Confession
because I couldn't even say
masturbation to the dark man
on the other side of the screen
three times as big as me. Or explain
how a girl could touch
herself and how it felt
good curling against the backs
of mis tías in the saggy bed.
Safe and hot in June.
On cool mornings, Nana would do
the long slow patting and rolling
of tortillas. I got browner,
ate *sopa*, stirred cinnamon sticks
into my Hershey's cocoa.
And the nights were soft,
like this lavendar powder
I bought at Woolworth's. Soft
nights when Mary y Pepita
would talk in their sleep
between me. I could hear

their dreams speaking
to each other. Dark words
flowing real easy through
the yellow curtain,
mis tías' faces
all smooth and brown.
Their eyelids would flutter
real delicate
above their dreams
and I would roll close
against them with nothing
to explain. Just words
spilling freely
from the mouths of sleeping girls.

Demetria Martínez

Crossing Over

"a sanctimonous band of renegades who advocate open violation of the law"
—Southwest Regional Commissioner for the U.S. Department of
Justice, Immigration and Naturalization Service on the sanctuary
movement

Somebody threw a baby
into the Río Grande River.

We scrub the scum off him
in the back of a station wagon
as we leave El Paso.
We tuck him, sleeping,
in a picnic basket
as we near the check point.
Officers see our fishing rods
and nod us through.
At midnight south of Albuquerque
we invent a name, a date of birth,
singing rock-a-bye-baby in English,
burying the placenta of his past.

2.
When Grandma left the Catholic Church
and joined Assemblies of God,
they dipped her in the Río Grande.
She stood up and cried.

Grandma, grandma, the river's not
the same. Sweet Jesus
got deported, this baby
bruised and hungry,
my nipples red and pained.

3.
Who's throwing babies
in the river?
What bastard
signs the release?

Who will break
the bastard's brains
and let this baby
keep his name?

Chimayo

Decked in October light adobe grows gold.
On one house a fresco of Jesus in thorns.
Red chiles strung by the decade,
Slung from porch beams.
Buckets of apples for sale.
Someone roasts green chile to peel and freeze.

Look, the Santuario de Chimayo,
Its steeples, like pencils
Sing the sky.
This is a pilgrimage, not a tour:
Make the sign of the cross.

Behind the church a mountain
Kneels in a field.
Sap on my fingers, plucking mushrooms
From timbers,
Someday when I sleep with you
It will taste like this.

Prologue: Salvadoran Woman's Lament

Nothing I do will take the war
out of my man.

A war without zones, soldiers raped
his sister at home—then disappeared him.

He returned, his rib cracked,
chest scorched with cigarettes.

The room spins at night, he says.
Last night I held him,

to keep him from falling,
he called me a whore.

When at last my man gets out
to become a new man in America,

when he finds a woman
to take the war out of him,

she will make love to a man
and a monster,

she will rise from the bed,
grenades ticking in her.

Nativity: For Two Salvadoran Women, 1986–87

Your eyes, large as Canada, welcome
this stranger.
We meet in a Juárez train station
where you sat for hours,
your offspring blooming in you
like cactus fruit,
dresses stained where breasts leak,
panties in purses tagged
"Hecho en El Salvador,"
your belts like equators,
mark north from south,
borders I cannot cross,
for I am an American reporter,
pen and notebook, the tools
of my tribe, distance us,
though in any other era I might
press a stethoscope to your wounds,
hear the symphony of the unborn,
finger forth infants to light,
wipe afterbirth, cut cords.

It is impossible to raise a child
in that country.

Sisters, I am no saint. Just a woman
who happens to be a reporter,
a reporter who happens
to be a woman,
squat in a forest, peeing
on pine needles,
watching you vomit morning sickness,
a sickness infinite as the war in El Salvador,
a sickness my pen and notebook will not ease,
tell me, *¿Por qué están aquí?*
How did you cross over?
In my country we sing of a baby in a manger,
finance death squads,
how to write of this shame,
of the children you chose to save?

It is impossible to raise a child
in that country.

A North American reporter,
I smile, you tell me you are due
in December, we nod,
knowing what women know.
I shut my notebook,
watch your car rock
through the Gila,
a canoe hanging over the windshield
like the beak of an eagle,
babies turning in your wombs,
summoned to Belén to be born.

Víctor Martínez

The Ledger

I suffer with song, yet I create them here on earth . . . — CUAOAHTZIN

I waited this long I might as well stay, I said
under my lapel to no one who could listen,
and took out my boyhood collection of June-bugs,
Yellow-jackets, and other species of wing
that slept once in my cotton pillow of alcohol
before freezing into decoration:
a mantis into prayer, a bee into a lifetime of work.

I remember baiting abdomens onto needles
to lure all eyes into my glass cases.
I caught salamander and bullfrog
to scuddle in my muddy tanks,
and when the hull of a sandcrab was a lesson
in form, a mere nothing on my palm,
its death was mine, and I recorded it in my ledger.

In my ledger, I wrote how a cat kneels
stiff under the fading thread of mice,
how winds splash the poplar and a sky opens
and pours milk into a river. I was there,
I stated how paralysis took my grandpa's tongue
and through it numbed everything, carried away
with the drool in the washbasin.

Because I took account, because I knew how
to put back the words, sponged from the slate,
I was his favorite, I was my family's best—
lugging around my book of events,
telling myself over and over into my collar
that this is all there is. This cold, flat
reduction of the living is all there is. And this too
I wrote down, and about the sidewalks glowing
with rain and neons, the streets hissing with cars.

Furniture

When the family upstairs moved away, I awoke in a bed
of morning, and sleep still weighing in my arms.
I knew it was me again, carrying out the furniture
from my grandmother's old house. And awake
I'm taken back to the narrow corridors of a room,
in a house abandoned, where night and morning
turn to embrace, without need of words
nor the thickness and punctuating gravity
of each footstep away from home.

Space explains itself in corner holes, in tiny murmurs
where speech resides.
They tell the story of a living room, of a grandfather
climbing up a trellis of opened books, of a grandmother
wandering again through the forests of her children
with only crumbs to lead her back, while life,
which was neither a rolling biological spiral,
nor the everyday occurrences burning out on the fringes
of dusk, devours them, hungry for more.

Today my arms are alive with the traces of leaves
reddening back to earth—alive, and still embracing a garden
of squash and bell peppers, tomatoes and *nopales*—
all the little vegetables I hold
in the warm kitchen of my lungs.

But again the walls of creation rise
as the worlds in children's crayon smear
before vanishing in the washcloth.
That is how we moved, taking everything, yet leaving more.
For a photo, we left a picture frame of dust.
For the seasons of travel, the distance pared from a heel.
Only these were left to speak
for the lives we only imagined.

Shoes

Out of all our enemies, all the catastrophes of nations
scattered to ash, plowed over with salt, we still have
the warm friendliness, the unrelenting spirit of our shoes to console us.

Two bubbles, chopped square out of a shapeless emptiness—
how this invention hisses in a hurry to correct time,
pumping little sneezes of sympathy for our tardiness.

Although they owe us nothing, they walk
in many of our dreams, conjuring music
from a vaporous sidewalk or standing
as pure reverence over the peaceful herds of our dead.

They, who always return back to us, faithfully,
from every tropic, every desert, to take up their jobs
as stealth for the burglar, spring under the killer's crouch,
courage for the guerrilla, nevertheless guard us against
thistles and thorns, protect us from stone and
the unseen disasters of glass.

Wheels mean nothing to the shoe.
They are the first of peasants, and would never think
to kneel before any god or suck up
to whatever tablet of the Law.

Shoes are ravenous for distance.
They supply whole lives
with the loss of a mere heel,
yet wear death, only once.

Some Things Left Unsaid

What can you say better than carcinoma?
Or the warty-eyed virus eating at the vocal cords?
The skies, the rivers and forests a brain dreams
get cut away by the same scalpel
that cuts away a malignant tumor.

Look at the boy who can't walk, the lipless girl,
the half-lung man.
There are words, but they mostly go unsaid
in EKG results, in the echoes after a sonogram
has sounded, in the worried ghost of an x-ray.

Over and over, in tomography charts, in bloody washbasins,
or the grave histories of lint beside the vacuum cleaner
something is talked out, perhaps explained, analyzed
or trusted to God.

But how do you speak about diseased blood?
How do you say,
when cancer spreads its arms inside your arms,
"I'm in love today," or "I'm going home."

But the sun passes over, or rather earth passes over the sun,
with its latest tally of diseases, bringing the light
that brailles another million new megabytes
on the computer disk of global massacres.
It's as if the horizon wants consistency above all,
above all a little consistency.

And so we are swept by the same wind that nourishes the leaves
for erasure.
But let our little children keep playing,
and the tongue of beef keep burbling in the clay pot;
all of creation just keeps spinning quietly on,
leaving everything unsaid.

All Is Well

I never need to see myself as I am in the mirror,
because nothing breathes there. I know already
every molecule,
because it is me who sticks a needle of light
through every pore and threads this life.

I talk into my collar to no one who could listen,
even the walls don't answer, nothing
in four directions, not even wind
nor an emptiness one can lean on or move against—

but then a string, attached to a window, and lashed
onto a wall of midnight, descends.
I hear the earth humming in airless space:
a globe on fire, with glaciers sliding into gorges
and valleys puddling with human larvae.

There are skies blown to cloudless shreds,
a crawling locust storm of diseases and infections
riffling like wind across a boar's hot bristly hide—

but down below, further down, where the tectonic stitches
burn, I see my mother stepping out the back porch
to hang the laundry. And above her, above her braided hair,
a landslide of nuclear wastes and unexploded bombs,
pinless and ready, are there
about to wash over her—

but then my father arrives, and together
they talk. She takes his hand. They kiss.
Two old people—they kiss—
because all is well.

Pat Mora

Gentle Communion

Even the long-dead are willing to move.
Without a word, she came with me from the desert.
Mornings she wanders through my rooms
making beds, folding socks.

Since she can't hear me anymore,
Mamande ignores the questions I never knew
to ask, about her younger days, her red
hair, the time she fell and broke her nose
in the snow. I will never know.

When I try to make her laugh,
to disprove her sad album face, she leaves
the room, resists me as she resisted
grinning for cameras, make-up, English.

While I write, she sits and prays,
feet apart, legs never crossed,
the blue housecoat buttoned high
as her hair dries white, girlish
around her head and shoulders.

She closes her eyes, bows her head,
and like a child presses her hands together,
her patient flesh steeple, the skin
worn, like the pages of her prayer book.

Sometimes I sit in her wide-armed
chair as I once sat in her lap.
Alone, we played a quiet *I Spy.*
She peeled grapes I still taste.

She removes the thin skin, places
the luminous coolness on my tongue.
I know not to bite or chew. I wait
for the thick melt,
our private green honey.

Rituals

Our children came for our hands,
for the last blessing, came to memorize our faces,
our wrinkled bark. One by one they returned to the *rancho*
on that grumbling bus. I felt the faces I no longer see,
traced eyebrows, nose, lips, gently pressed their eyelids,
felt their life flicker on my fingertips.

The house was noisy again, the arguing, loud pigeons
flapping. My husband shouted orders, missing the sound
of his own voice. He showed our sons the bags of cement
to seal us on all sides so we will lie clean in that hole.
He sent the youngest to Santa María for the coffins,
said to store corn and beans in them until we die.
A safe, dry place. He gave our sons his hoe and pick,
but said, "*Oigan, muchachos.* I know my young one
drinks too much beer. Touch him and no locks will keep me out."

My startled birds left the thorny nest again.
My husband is all bones now, even cotton pants wear him out.
All day we linger at our door. My days are nights.
I've learned to feel my way.

Señora X No More

Straight as a nun I sit.
My fingers foolish before paper and pen
hide in my palms. I hear the slow, accented echo
   How are yu? I ahm fine. How are yu?
of the other women who clutch notebooks and blush
at their stiff lips resting
sounds that float graceful as
bubbles from their children's mouths.
My teacher bends over me, gently squeezes
my shoulders, the squeeze I give my sons,
hands louder than words.
She slides her arms around me:
a warm shawl, lifts my left arm
onto the cold, lined paper.
"Señora, don't let it slip away," she says
and opens the ugly, soap-wrinkled fingers of my right hand
with a pen like I pry open the lips of a stubborn grandchild.
My hand cramps around the thin hardness.
"Let it breathe," says this woman who knows
my hand and tongue knot, but she guides
and I dig the tip of my pen into that white.
I carve my crooked name, and again at night

until my hand and arm are sore,
I carve my crooked name,
my name.

Arte Popular

A hot breath among the pale crystal,
and polite watercolors of this tidy museum,
a breathing
in these new rooms,
and   faint drums, whistles, chants.

Judas figures puffed with sins
rise to the ceiling ready to explode
into pure white smoke,
dragons' eyes bulge,
and green claws reach to pull your hair
as masks sneer down
at skeletons dressed as bride and groom.

                In Mexican villages
                wrinkled hands lure and trap
                dark spirits,
                snakes
                        slide into woven reeds
                dogs
                        growl softly in wood
                frogs
                        blow their wet song into clay flutes

                    jaguars
                        pant in papier-mâché
a breathing   those spirits poised
to inhale deeply, fly out museum windows,
leap down steps three at a time, slither
on cool white marble into the night, into the full moon.

Judith Ortiz Cofer

The Dream of Birth

My mother's voice scrapes the ocean floor,
coming through ragged with static during the call
placed from her sister's house in Puerto Rico,
   where she will stay
until she finds a new place for herself. She has called
to say she is moving again and to share the horror
prompting her flight.

On the first night of deep sleep in the old house
she had rented back on native soil—a place
she would decorate with our past; where

yellowed photographs—of a young man in khaki
army issue (the way she chooses to remember her husband),
and my brother and me as sepia-toned babies—in their

chipped frames, will not insult new paint; a place
where she could finally begin to collect
her memories like jars of preserves on a shelf,
                                          there,
she had laid down to rest on her poster bed centered in
a high-ceilinged room, exhausted from the labor
of her passage, and dreamed

she had given birth to one of us again; she felt the weight
of a moist, wriggling mass on her chest, the greedy mouth
seeking a milk-heavy breast, then suddenly—real pain—

piercing as a newborn infant's cry—yanking her
out of her dream. In the dark she felt the awful heft
of the thing stirring over her, flipping on the light,

she saw, to her horror, a bat clinging to her gown,
its hallucinated eyes staring up from the shroud of black wings,
hanging on with perfect little fingers,
                                                    as she,
wild with fear and revulsion, struggled free of her clothes,
throwing the bundle hard against the wall. By daylight
she had returned to find the rust-colored stain streaked

on the white plaster, and the thing still fluttering
in the belly of the dress. She had dug a tiny grave
with her gardening spade on the spot

where she would have planted roses.

The Latin Deli

Presiding over a Formica counter,
plastic Mother and Child magnetized
to the top of an ancient register,
the heady mix of smells from the open bins
of dried codfish, the green plantains
hanging in stalks like votive offerings,
she is the Patroness of Exiles,
a woman of no-age who was never pretty,
who spends her days selling canned memories
while listening patiently to the Puerto Ricans complain
that it would be cheaper to fly to San Juan

than to buy a pound of Bustelo coffee here,
and to Cubans perfecting their speech
of a "glorious return" to Havana—where no one
has been allowed to die and nothing to change until then;
to Mexicans who pass through, talking lyrically
of *dólares* to be made in El Norte—
                              all wanting the comfort
of spoken Spanish, to gaze upon the family portrait
of her plain wide face, her ample bosom
resting on her plump arms, her look of maternal interest
as they speak to her and each other
of their dreams and their disillusions—
how she smiles understanding,
when they walk down the narrow aisles of her store
reading the labels of packages aloud, as if
they were the names of lost lovers: *Suspiros*,
Merengues, the stale candy of everyone's childhood.
                              She spends her days
slicing *jamón y queso* and wrapping it in wax paper
tied with string: plain ham and cheese
that would cost less at the A&P, but it would not satisfy
the hunger of the fragile old man lost in the folds
of his winter coat, who brings her lists of items
that he reads to her like poetry, or the others,
whose needs she must divine, conjuring up products
from places that now exist only in their hearts—
closed ports she must trade with.

Saint Rose of Lima

"Never let my hands be to anyone an occasion for temptation."— ISABEL DE FLORES

She was the joke of the angels—a girl
crazy enough for God

that she despised her own beauty; who grew bitter herbs
to mix with her food,

who pinned a garland of roses to her forehead;
and who, in a fury of desire

concocted a potion of Indian pepper and bark
and rubbed it on her face, neck, and breasts

disfiguring herself.
Then, locked away in a dark cell,

where no reflection is possible,
she begged for death to join her with her Master

whom she called, *Divine Bridegroom, Thorn
in my Heart, Eternal Spouse.*

She would see His vague outline, feel His cool touch
on her fevered brow,

but as relief came, her vision would begin to fade,
and once again she would dip the iron bar into the coals,

and pass it gently like a magician's wand over her skin—
to feel the passion that flames up for a moment,

in all dying things.

Fever

Father was to her, and to me,
like the wind—blowing through our house
on weekend leaves—and when we spoke to him,
he carried our voices away.

When he left,
and silence grew inside my mother like a child,
I would watch as she set the table for two,
then ate by herself in the kitchen, standing.

And she taught me this:
that silence is a thick and dark curtain,
the kind that pulls down over a shop window;

that love is the quick repercussion of a stone
bouncing off the same darkened window; that pain
is something you embrace, like a rag doll
no one will ask you to share.

Some nights, she allowed me in her bed.
Her skin was as cool as the surface
of the pillow the sick child clings to, awakening
from feverish dreams.

I would lay my head close to hers and listen
to the fine, knotted thread of her breath,
to her rosary of sighs,

her peace so deepened by sorrow, I know
it sustained me then, as the light
slipping past heavy, dark curtains might nourish
a small plant set, by accident, close

to the window.

Vida

My lover is the old poet, Gabriel,
who lives on a mountain, high above the rest of us—
in the place, he says, where sadness makes its nest,
where time is very long.

The day begins, Gabriel writes his ailments for an age,
then night comes like a thief dressed in black.

Sometimes, when the moon is bright enough,
I climb the rocky hill to his house.
He is always waiting at the window—for me or for daybreak;
I don't ask. He knows he has little time left,
and will not waste it on sleep.

When I hold this old man in my arms,
his thin body light as bird-bones, I feel
as if I were warming a wounded sparrow. From his gray eyes
little light comes. And I know
that he is now writing words for the stone carver.

Before autumn, I will be gathering flowers for his grave:
a basketful of Bird-of-Paradise,
the ones he once called in a poem
a flock of yellow-crested cockateels. I will pick
Flame-of-the-Forest, the burning orange blossom
he likes to see in my black hair.

I will spread them over the little square of earth
he has himself chosen: at the point where sky touches ground
and a Kapok tree has offered him shade
for half a century. There he has often rested his head
on the lap of its smooth trunk, to watch
the little wild parrots alight at dusk, greening the branches
like new leaves; there too he has listened
to their murmurings until darkness silenced them.

But on this night, he will welcome me with wine and flowers.
He will call me mi vida—his life.
I will keep him company until the sun rises over the mountain.

The Campesino's Lament

It is Ash Wednesday and Christ is waiting
to die. I have left my fields dark and moist
with last night's rain to take the sacrament.
My face is streaked with ashes. Come back,
mujer. Without you,
                    I am an empty place
where spiders crawl and nothing takes root.
Today, taking the Host, I remembered your hands,
incense and earth, fingertips like white grapes
I would take into my mouth
one by one.
                  When I enter the house,
it resists me like an angry woman. Our room,
your things, the bed—a penance I offer up for Lent.
In sweet mango breaths. Watching you sleep,
I willed my dreams into you.

But clouds cannot be harvested, nor children wished
into life.
                  In the wind that may travel
as far as you have gone, I send this message: out here,
in a place that you will not forget, a simple man
has been moved to curse the rising sun, and to question
God's unfinished work.

Leroy Quintana

Grandfather Never Wrote a Will

Grandfather never wrote a will
Simply told Don Ricardo the house was to be mine
A man's word, nothing else
though Don Ricardo said few at the funeral
Spoke the language silent men speak
I did not understand then
I spoke only the language of the university
In his old age, long after his only child, a son,
has died, I suppose Don Ricardo endured, home late
each night with Doña María, after the bar closed,
in the town's only taxi
Grandfather's house became nothing more than memories
A place family continues to fight each other for

After Her Husband Died,
Doña Carlota Was So Alone

After her husband died, Doña Carlota was so alone
she wanted nothing more than to die
One day she decided how she would end her life:
leave the gas on
After fixing some tortillas, frijoles for her son
to eat when he arrived home from work
But as she turned a tortilla over she beheld
the image of her husband scorched on it

A sign from God she should live,
spend the rest of her days in peace
The tortilla I am told is in her living room
next to a photo of her dearly-departed Esteban
so unbelievingly striking in resemblance,
preserved forever in Saran Wrap

Grandmother's Father Was Killed by Some Tejanos

Grandmother's father was killed by some Tejanos
one winter, hit in the back of the head with a rifle butt
as he was placing his foot into some tracks in the snow
to prove they were too big to be his
They had accused him of stealing traps from their lines
One of grandmother's brothers had to be restrained
from emptying his rifle in anger

After the trial, when the verdict was given
the Tejanos flung their hats
and emptied their rifles into the sky

Of all the stories Grandma told me
I wonder why she never mentioned
a word of this to me and whether or not
I should and if so how
to tell my children who gather round the TV
the way I sat with Grandma
summer evenings on the backyard patio
winters as she spun sugar candy on the firewood stove

Granizo

To have been gone so long
But to have forgotten hail,
its name in Spanish, *granizo*,
until a storm, as I drove
toward a place named Golondrinas,
eight miles from the main highway
because I was enchanted by the name
I was home again,
if only for a while, after eighteen years
I remembered grandfather, his cornfield
Somehow granizo belongs to him
He named it each summer
as he sat and watched, defined its terror
An old enemy, the way only water,
if it isn't gentle rain, can be

Antonia Quintana Pigño

La Jornada

"My two great loves are physics and New Mexico. It's a pity they can't be combined."

—J. R. OPPENHEIMER

Oppenheimer
I could have loved you
wrapped my legs tightly
around your white buttocks
to keep you thinly against me
without desire
      for food
      for water from mountain streams
for the journey to Jornada del Muerto
for the creation of Trinity

I would have met you along
the ridge of Frijoles Canyon
caught breathless by your intensity
and sad eyes
      your boyish dishevelment
would have seduced me
to seduce you
just clumsily enough
to surprise and charm you
away from quantum mechanics
the enigmatic half-life of identical nuclei
and the gray uniform houses of Los Álamos

at least for awhile

until the 14th passed and the 15th
and the 16th
defying the test that would test us all.

Before the red dawn
I would have awakened beside you
untangled myself in that narrow bed
to slide on top of you
onto you
and whisper only for you

mi Nuevo Méjico
Love   listen
the children are singing
as they taxi along the dirt road
back and forth on the broken bicycle.
They think they share heaven
"no tornadoes, no hurricanes,
we're so lucky," they say
in singsong Mexican accents
and do you know?
¿Sabes, mi Roberto,
that my father couldn't stay in California
even for sweet warm thick slices
of 5¢ watermelon
pleasures of avocados
ripe oranges and lemons
right off the tree
and a steady government job
on the docks
so without word

piled us all into the Model A
the new baby born in San Francisco
and drove back to pumping gas,
fixing flats, dirt floors
and drinking cerveza with his compadres
He liked land brown
and familiar like him
afternoons burned into
the skin by sun—
his legacy to us, to me, in me?

And riding in me the passion of New Mexico
up to mountain streams and ruins without names
on the bed of an old pickup
sleeping within me the desire
to empower poetry with the very physics
of the land
            Consider   querido mío

        poetry—

            how it changes only
                perception

not the land:

        A gust of wind whips a-
            round the corner
            of the jr high
            where two girls walk-
                backward

                    whips
            at their backs
                    lifts
        their skirts
                    blows
stinging sand against
the slight curve of bare thighs
        they chatter
        and lick ice-cream cones
        harbored in still coves
                made by the slight curve
                of slender shoulders

You could have held me by the poetry
of Classical Analysis
spoken Sanskrit verses to me
upon the ruins of the high adobe city of Puye
where ancient
we would gaze beyond Black Mesa
at the blue haze of the mountain range
ranging from the Colorado Sangre de Cristos
clear south
to the Sandías
and then, the Manzanos
but your passion was physics, the fission
of it and separation never scared you
not even my sad eyes
Don't look at me like I'm leaving you and
            your eight children
and a small kiss upon my cheek before you left
leaving me lost in crumpled linen.
I couldn't have stopped your drive through all those summers
with your family in Christ's blood red mountains where you

learned to love your version of the air I couldn't have
stopped your drive past Santa Fe Albuquerque Isleta Belén
slipping left after Socorro into the light of a new world.

Vicente

She is dead at twenty-seven.
Her father's ranch is in the valley, visible from the Los
    Lunas hills
            where she is being buried.
East lie the dark blue Manzanos. The summer morning is fresh
    and clear—
            green elms, sweet air, brown earth.
In town her husband sits in his cell.
In spring he will hang himself.

I have just returned from seeing Vicente. He hardly
    recognized me
            through the small barred opening of the iron door.
"Is this Daniela, Mama? Is this Daniela?"
"Sí, m'hijo."
I hardly know him—he is thin, grown too thin—Mama has
    brought young
            Tito's levis. Only a few weeks ago he was
    muscular, strong.
In jail for killing his wife.

Outside our house in Albuquerque Father sits beneath a tree
    on a straight
            backed chair-blue work shirt, khaki pants, one leg
    crossed

over the other, brown work boots.
I find him talking to a friend. Finishing the story, he
    adds,
        "Pobrecito, pobrecito hijo."
The friend sees me, says nothing and lowering his eyes looks
    away.

Tito and I take the boys to Dairy Queen. Memo's face swells
        with laughter.
Chrisy laughs too.
I wonder how he thinks of that day, the ranch, his father,
    his mother,
        the gun.
They laugh and spill ice cream in the car.
We tease them, filling them with more and more.
The sticky baby falls asleep.

In autumn it is settled. Julio, the eldest brother, will
    hire the
        lawyer, Father's knees ache—he barely walks.
The father-in-law coffees daily with the jailers and
    continues legal
        proceedings for custody of the boys.

Thinner still, Vicente sits in Los Lunas and waits.

Mama, spurned by St. Anne's, argues that as a Marine he
    deserves burial
        in the National Cemetery.
In summer the boys move to the Los Lunas ranch.

Years later, I visit the Santa Fe National Cemetery for the
    first time.
The woman in the office inquires, "What is his name?"
The routine manner, the present tense and he is briefly alive

The section where he's buried is being watered to keep the
    grass
            richly green in the sandy soil, the stone markers
    are
            white, the sky blue and to the east, the Sangre de
    Cristos.

Outside the entrance to the cemetery is a *camposanto*. These
    are the graves of those whose heroes lie buried within
    the formal gates.
The graves are dirt mounds, some covered by gray-leaved weeds
    with
    tiny purple flowers, some encircled by round stones,
    others
    decorated with fading homemade paper flowers.
Wooden and iron railings enclose the graves of the infants.
Markers are weathered wooden crosses and small glass-covered
    cards
            whose names and dates have been bleached away by the
    sun.

A young man in a small vehicle approaches the area to turn
    off the
            sprinkler system.
My shoes are wet when I reach the grave.
Engraved on the stone, his name, his dates, his term of
    military service.
I read no further, I remember the story.

December's Picture

"Las Manitas is a very old Spanish house with several patios and roof levels. Many additions indicate portions were built in the 1700's."
— Illustrated Historical Calender for Bernalillo County, NM 1976

He wondered why
his sister had sent
the calendar.
Maybe you'd like
to frame December?

Under oil gray skies
brown adobe walls
stand silent
trimmed with snow.

Era la casa de tus abuelos.

Curved earth walls flank
steps to a rooftop where
once a profusion of chiles lay
like warm red tiles in the sun.
Beyond ribboned windows of iron
whorls—a possibility of lace
and somewhere
a chimney sends
scents of warmth
and roasting pinones.

This was the house of our abuelos.

He watched his mother
shape the tortilla
her floured hands turning
the widening white circle.
He wondered if
she gave away her silks
her laces
and taking leave
touched the leaves
the branches
smooth walls of adobe
which enclosed
her father's garden,
if she turned and moved slowly
across the Old Town Bridge
to be with the young coal miner
from Madrid.
He wondered and thought to ask
but saw
already in her eyes
the silence of winter snow.

Naomi Quiñónez

Hesitations

I laugh
a glass of wine
between my legs,
dark, intensely burgundy,
glows from the warmth of my thighs.

I stare
into that crystal glass,
wait for it to reveal
past and future.
A fortuneteller
staring into herself
and finding nothing.

I feel
the tight vacuum of my womanhood
compressed
and kept between my legs
for no one to see,
for someone to anticipate,
for no one to see.

I am my own chastity belt,
and I laugh at that thought
into the dark red wine
that tells me nothing.

Before I grow confused,
and crush the glass
with my thighs,
I laugh again,
I look again
bring the wine to my lips
and take a long drink.

My Shattered Sister

Sister, I wish to be the waters
of insistent rivers
the long arms of the Colorado
that reach past those man-made borders
to the surging Amazon currents.
Is not your blood my blood
whether coursing through veins
of family I have never met
or spilled on the land
of a continent we share?
My blood is yours,
we are the bleeding twins.
You are the southern sister
veiled in oppressive shadow
that covers your enigmatic light,
I, the Northern twin,
watch angrily
with fists clenched tight
the cancer that invades
our ancestors' defiled dreams.
Your cries become deafening

as the distance disappears.
Deserts burn,
jungles part silent,
your broken body
appears before me
in a paid advertisement
on the 11 o'clock news
as you break the zombie stupor
of televised distraction.
You are the drumming noise
of my sleepless nights.
The dancing voices of children
become a mother's anguished cries
and ricochet off
the prefabricated fortresses
we have so carefully constructed.
You haunt me sister
when I pretend
it could never happen here
or as I turn the pages
and read the countless headlines:
Latino family of 12 living in 2-room shack,
Health care denied campesinos,
Latino unemployment doubles.
Somewhere a warm wind whirls
past our neon-lit hopes,
it is your breath sister
carrying the scent
of ashes and blood
as your voice becomes the river
that connects us.
And we all walk quieter

in the clutches of the North
when we hear the splintered echoes
of America to the South.

People of the Harvest

The crushed grape
withers on the vine
no gnarled hands to pick it
no one to make wine.
Lettuce now lost
wilts on its row
the empty fields forgotten
by scythe and sickle and hoe.
Cotton worms slowly
drying in the sun
if there were backs
to carry it
but there are none.
Fruit long past ripe
falls heavy to the ground
and bursts its rotting entrails
with a sluggish sound.
The fields are all in mourning
rotting blackly
in their sorrow
for the people of the harvest
who will not return tomorrow.
The grapevine now a gravemark
for every back-wrenched soul
that spent a life of labor

and died
giving birth to growth.
The poison that protects the field
often kills the worker.
The sun that ignites
orchards to bloom
beats hard upon the child
and sucks life away.
When the field has finished rotting
and gives herself to bloom
be aware of the many souls
in the orchard's perfume
in the fine green skin of the plant
in the sweetness of the fruit
in the soil dark
with my people's blood
in the fiber
of the root.

America's Wailing Wall

There was a sixties hitch
and we were it.
The world around us
launched an all-out defensive
and you were sent to
screaming eagles.
I defied tradition.
There was movement
and we pushed hard
against new skin.

Out here the world
was a carnival
of blind purpose
and anger.
The striated hues
of social change
became vivid
and finally
bold with reason.
In your twilight zone
of death
you drained
into pale submission.
The moss green
of your jacket
a fibrous tumor
on your good spirit.
A blood belt of outrage
bonded us
before the barrios
became a pond
fat with fish
for military consumption.
"Carnal"
I named you affectionately
"Carnalita" you responded.
Each day
one more young man
disappeared off the streets,
hooked on the bait
dropped before carnales like you.
Jail or war
Poverty or war

Victim of war
Later your letters appeared.
Words lined the pages
like tired weeds.
I answered
giving all the details
for my life of infamy
describing my own war
of wombs and justice.
You gave me few clues
but your letters
smelled of death
and between the stiff
upper lip
of your lines
I read your daily horrors.

Today I walk to the wall
we have constructed for you
the thousands of names
solidified
into a polished monolith.
Your name stands there
someplace
between millions of names
of those
sentenced to death.

Alberto Ríos

I Would Visit Him in the Corner

He was the uncle who when he was young
and lying down had a spider crawl
into the large hole of his left ear and stay

through the night. Even after it was crushed
on the side of the head and he saw the legs
he never could believe it was gone

and so that ear was always stopped up
even though he would stand sometimes
like a swimmer jumping up and down

with his head cocked. It kept him from dying
in the war because they would not take him.
But he said he died anyway, and had nightmares

that crawled. And his ear grew bigger
because he kept hitting it, and when he was old
it became his habit, even when it bled.

Finally in the red night scratching
with no one to see and nothing to hold
the spider carelessly left him.

Saints, and Their Care

Doña Gabriela made the front
    and biggest room of the house green
As a practical matter and in homage to
The fine framed picture of the painting
La Virgen de Guadalupe, and its coloration
    with which everyone is familiar
As she appeared to Juan Diego the Indian.
The white doilies on the green chairs furthermore
Made a pleasing contrast
With or without their having any inner knowledge
    of the presence of the picture in the room,
The doilies with their lace aspect
    looking like something one supposes
The Virgin must have worn, or desired to wear,
A color she wept from her eyes
Though the picture of the painting did not show it.
Green was her color, but white was her desire:
In her eyes, the way the pupils and irises
    were all business
But then all of the white to the sides
    being what she did in her leisure time
    after supper, after taking care of the dogs
    and having covered the parrot for sleep.
She was a saint, and this is their way,
    thought Doña Gabriela as she was finished
    with all of the pieces of the room.
To make one look only into the center of their eyes.

The Purpose of Altar Boys

Tonio told me at catechism
the big part of the eye
admits good, and the little
black part is for seeing
evil—his mother told him
who was a widow and so
an authority on such things.
That's why at night
the black part gets bigger.
That's why kids can't go out
at night, and at night
girls take off their clothes
and walk around their
bedrooms or jump on their
beds or wear only sandals
and stand in their windows.
I was the altar boy
who knew about these things,
whose mission on some Sundays
was to remind people of
the night before as they
knelt for Holy Communion.
To keep Christ from falling
I held the metal plate
under chins, while on the thick
red carpet of the altar
I dragged my feet
and waited for the precise
moment: plate to chin
I delivered without expression

the Holy Electric Shock,
the kind that produces
a really large swallowing
and makes people think.
I thought of it as justice.
But on other Sundays the fire
in my eyes was different,
my mission somehow changed.
I would hold the metal plate
a little too hard
against those certain same
nervous chins, and I,
I would look
with authority down
the tops of white dresses.

The Good Lunch of Oceans

I ate with my father
The avocado
And thought without telling him
The skin of a sidewalk
Dirty with stones. It is the
Harbor line of Thrill
And the swim inside.
Scrotum skin,
I could not tell him.
How its feel was of sutures
Holding the body together
At its very base.
            Green meat,

Feel of sand completely
Wet, a fragile
Lip meat, mouth
Meat of dreams
Two places on her body.
          Green in a garden
Of celeries and the lost
Cat-eye marble
That won me everything.
Old Chevrolet paint, green
Virgin of Guadalupe,
That famous painting
The color of the Thirties,
From which deep orange
Has also survived. Green
That used to be green.
          Failed ocarina
Little bear
Shape of an ocean,
I eat our avocado
With my father, play
For its music
In my mouth.

Lost on September Trail, 1967

There was a roof over our heads
and that was at least something.
Then came dances.
The energy for them came from
childhood, or before, from the time

when only warmth was important.
We had come to the New World
and become part of it.
If the roof would shelter us,
we would keep it in repair.
Roof then could be roof,
solid, visible, recognizable,
and we could be whatever it was
that we were at this moment.
Having lost our previous names
somewhere in the rocks we ran,
we could not yet describe ourselves.
For two days the rain had been
steady, and we left the trail
because one of us remembered
this place. Once when I was young
I had yielded to the temptation
of getting drunk, and parts of it
felt like this, wet and hot,
timeless, in the care of someone
else. After the dances we sat
like cubs, and cried for that
which in another world might be
milk, but none came.
We had only ourselves, side by side
and we began a wrestling
that comes, like dances, out of
nowhere and leaves into the night
like sophisticated daughters
painted and in plumes, but young,
a night darker than its name.
We gave ourselves over in adoration
of the moon, but we did not call it

moon, the words that came out
were instead noises as we tried
to coax it close enough
to where we might jump,
overpower it, and bring it to our
mouths, which is, after all,
the final test of all things.
But we could not, it only circled us,
calmly, and we wanted it more.
We called it Carlos, but it did not
come, we called it friend, comrade,
with our eyes open, not trusting
each other, dark pushing us even
farther into childhood, into liquid,
making us crave eyelessness,
craving so hard we understand
prayer without knowing its name.
At some point failing
ourselves, eyelids fell.
We dreamt the dream of farther
worlds, so different they cannot
be remembered, cannot be remembered
because they cannot be described
or even imagined. We woke
and did not remember, and the night
before became part of us
and we did not remember
speaking to the moon.
We got up from the years without numbers
and called
each other by name.
Honey, the one that was me said,
drying her tears that were

really the rain from the night
before, which had taken her
without me knowing, *honey*,
again, but she did not understand.
She wanted only the sun
because she was cold, she pulled out
hair to offer it, from her head
and offered now me
more of herself. I took it.
I put it in my mouth,
put it to a cupped tongue
and took it in. She moved
and I put my hands on her knees
which looked up at opposite ends
of the sky.

Luis J. Rodríguez

The Blast Furnace

A foundry's stench, the rolling mill's clamor,
the jack hammer's concerto leaving traces
between worn ears. Oh sing me a bucket shop blues
under an accordian's spell
with blood notes cutting through the black air
for the working life, for the rotating shifts
for the day's diminishment and rebirth.
The lead seeps into your skin like rainwater
along stucco walls; it blends into the fabric of cells,
the chemistry of bone, like a poisoned paintbrush
coloring skies of smoke, devouring like a worm
that never dies, a fire that's never quenched.
The blast furnace bellows out a merciless melody
as molten metal runs red down your back,
as assembly lines continue rumbling
into your brain, into forever,
while rolls of pipes crash onto brick floors.
The blast furnace spews a lava of insipid dreams,
a deathly swirl of screams; of late night wars
with a woman, a child's book of fear,
a hunger of touch, a hunger of poetry,
a daughter's hunger for laughter.
It is the sweat of running, of making love,
a penitence pouring into ladles of slag.
It is falling through the eyes of a whore,
a red-core bowel of rot,
a red-eyed train of refugees,

a red-scarred hand of unforgiveness,
a red-smeared face of spit.
It is blasting a bullet through your brain,
the last dying echo of one who enters
the volcano's mouth to melt.

Tomatoes

When you bite
deep to the core
of a ripe, juicy tomato,
sing a psalm
for Margarito Lupercio.

Praise the 17-year existence
of an immigrant tomato picker.

But don't bother to look
for his fingerprints
on the thin tomato skins.

They are implanted
on the banks
of the Delta Mendota Canal,
imbedded on soft soil
where desperate fingers
grasped and pulled,
reaching out
to silent shadows on shore
as deadly jaws

of rushing water
pulled him to its belly.

Margarito had jumped in,
so he could keep working;
to escape,
            miserly taunts,
            stares of disdain;
            indignities of alienhood
to escape,
            Border Patrol officers tearing across
            a tomato field like cowboys,
to escape,
            the iron bars of desert cells
            and hunger's dried-up face.

A brother of the fields
heard Margarito's cries
as the Migra officers watched
and did nothing.

He tied together torn sheets,
shirts, loose rope—
anything he could find,
pleading for help
in the anxious tones
that overcome language barriers.

Officers, in your name,
watched
and did nothing.

Workers later found Margarito's body
wedged in the entrails
of a sluice gate.
They delivered it to town,
tomato capital of the world,
awakened now, suddenly
to the tyranny of indifference.

Juchitán

1.
In the *zócalo*, the banter
of black birds rises
as the afternoon rolls in
and people come to gather.

This is a place
so removed from home—and so close.
Of tropical scents,
brightly colored *huipiles*
and an ancient language
whispered by children at play,
women relating the news
and drunks brawling over obscure points.

An odor of beef heads—eyes bulging—
cooking in open *taco* stands
satiates the humid air.
Tehuanas, wide Indian women
with hearty laughs and round faces,

prepare fish and iguanas
for the marketplace.

I slice a path
through the dampness,
the children's laughter
and singing of black birds.

2.
White metal benches
fill with young lovers,
the elderly
and sleepy-eyed.
Teenagers scamper by in T-shirts that say:
Juchitán: *Capital del Mundo*—
Juchitán: Capitol of the World.

Every scraped eye,
every hungry cry,
finds shape in Juchitán.
Every oppressor's fear,
every liberator's spear,
is alive in Juchitán.

Harried merchants call to one another.
A young mother pokes out a brown breast.
Across the street, government troops
calmly cradle machine guns.

3.
A pile of rocks
lie near a large bell
on top of the municipal palace.

From here, the movement
of troops is studied.
At signs of attack
the bell is to be tolled—
to call out *tecos*
from farms, homes and the marketplace.
They have no weapons.
Save sticks. Save rocks.

The voting is today.
Government supporters have beaten
two foreign journalists, accused of truth.
Truckloads of paid voters
come in shifts from nearby towns.
The *tecos* march on muddy paths,
past thatched-roofed huts,
in protest.
Late at night, troops move closer.
I'm stuck on the *palacio's* third floor.
Next to the bell.
Journalists are told to leave.
I pick up a rock.

4.
"They're going to kill you,"
a taxi driver informs me.
It's 4A.M.
All night long, the government ruling party
held feasts. Armed guards
protected their revelry.
The government has stolen the elections.
Thousands of *tecos*
assemble at the *palacio* to hear

their defeated representatives,
in the music of the Zapoteca tongue,
hold high their centuries-old
war of liberation.

"I know," I tell the taxi driver,
"but take me to the bus station anyway."
It's not safe for sympathetic "gringos"
(even if brown) to stay around
I carry the *Juchitecos* struggle
in a journal and in film.

The taxi driver looks at me hard
—then laughs.
"You must be crazier than I am,"
and takes my bag. I clinch the camera.
A lone pig wobbles along a dirt road.

Every Breath a Prayer

San Quentin, Baja California, 1983

Fernando, *el mixteco*,
climbs the red dirt of baja hills
along rain-drenched paths
through a field of waist-high grass.
He stops at a clearing where a rainbow
of piled stones,
colored sticks and flowers
share communion with the ground

of the living
to the ground of the dead.

Dozens of baby graves fill the hillside;
little ones in shoebox-size coffins
adorned with painted rock, sea shells
and wooden crosses, sprinkled with dry leaves,
and buried near the tomato plants
where some 80,000
Mixteco Indians are seasonally
enslaved.

Fernando, *el mixteco*,
leaves his plastic and carton shack
and passes an old irrigation pump
where his three-year-old boy
was crushed in the mesh of steel gears
on a Sunday of play.

Fernando crisscrosses
the sutured earth
alongside the fires that light
the glazed faces of mothers
squatting with diseased children
in the heart of dust.

He steps across a rotting plank
used as a bridge over a stream
as a woman leans over
pushing rags wet against the rocks
and another nearby
pressing a crusted nipple

to the mouth of a baby;
its every breath, a prayer.

Fernando, *el mixteco*,
then eyes the north
where a wind comes and ruffles
his thick hair
as he declares death to death,
his eyes dark with
the hollow of unborn days.

Fernando's body becomes the sides
of a native dirt-brick house,
his hair turns into a tarred-paper
and branched roof;
an arm becomes a child becomes home.

Leo Romero

If Marilyn Monroe

If Marilyn Monroe
had been an Indian
would she have still
been considered
sexy
And would she
have become
a movie star
perhaps playing
the part
of a squaw
being raped
and massacred
over and over
in movie after movie
with many close ups
of bare breasts
and thighs
Would her hair
still have been
as golden
And would every man
in America
have wanted
to make love
to her
when their wives

weren't looking
Would she still
have made teenage
boys
grow old with longing
even if she spoke
in a tongue
no white man
could understand
and had ancestral
memories
of being driven
into a tiny corner
of America
Would America
have forgiven itself
for what it did
to this Indian
Marilyn Monroe

Pito, I Say

Pito, I say
The wine does flow
And Pito says, it does
flow under the bridge
and the barges do flow
on it, and the wine
does flow
and the world flows away
Sure, I say

that's how it is
and Diane Arbus, I say
have you dreamt of her
lately
Lately, as not, says Pito
I dream of her constantly
I don't know if it's real
or not, he says
I envy you, I say
And you with real women, he says
She's just a dream
woman, he says
It's all a dream, I say
Life is all dreams, I say
And Diane, I say
How is it with her
It's good, Pito says, it's good
Is that real, I say
It's as real as a dream can be
Pito says

Time Is What You Make of It

Time is what you make of it
I say to Pito, Pito looks
at me disgusted like, Like
he does most time, Time is
good times, I say, Say what?
says Pito, Time plus time
I say, equals good times
You're crazy, says Pito, Pito

I say, I love time like a lady
Where are the breasts of time
yells Pito, Where are the thighs
of time, yells Pito, There is
no time like a lady, yells Pito
Time, I insist to Pito, is what
you make of it, It makes of you
what it will, yells Pito
And a fool is what I see it's
making of you, says Pito
Pito, I say, You're my friend
Time is what I like to spend
with my friends, I say
Pito gets up to leave, I got
no more time to waste, says Pito
Time's not wasted on friends
I say, Pito looks at me as if
he were about to shoot me
I'm leaving, he says, I had
a good time, I yell after him
But he don't turn around
I walk to the refrigerator
and get a beer and think to myself
I got time today to do as I please
I sit down and enjoy my time
It's another good time happening
I think to myself and take
another drink of cold beer

In This Dream, Pito and

In this dream, Pito and
Diane Arbus go out
for a cup of decaf
and a roll some place
You're not drinking
your coffee, Pito says
That's OK, says Diane
I just want to hear
you talk, How about
your roll, says Pito
You eating that
No, you can have it
says Diane, I'm too sick
to eat
Sick of what, says Pito
The doctors don't know
she says, I think it's
the birth control pills
and the hepatitis
I had once
So, you're taking
the pill, says Pito
looking at Diane intently
I've lost eight pounds
says Diane as she fidgets
with the lens on one
of her cameras
You wear those cameras
around your neck
as if they were charms

or holy medals, says Pito
Diane looks up at him
and smiles wryly, Maybe
they are, she says
You're the sexiest woman
I've ever known, says
Pito craning his neck
She's let her minidress
slide back far enough
for him to see her panties
And then Pito is blinded
by the flash of Diane's
camera
Not again, says Pito
Diane keeps clicking her
camera, she gets up
and takes shots of him
from all different angles
I don't like you taking
my picture, says Pito
Not tonight
But Diane doesn't listen
Not tonight
But Diane doesn't listen
She's possessed
Click, flash, click, flash
You're blinding me, Pito yells
And when he wakes up
the bright light of morning
is hitting him in the face
and he's in bed, alone

In This Dream, I Drop By

In this dream, I drop by
at Pito's with Diane
Pito, I say, this is Diane
Arbus, the famous photographer
I know, says Pito, we already
met, Hello, Pito, says Diane
smiling at him as if they're
old friends, I turn to Diane
Why didn't you say anything
I say, She doesn't answer me
She just looks at me and smiles
Pito has a great place
don't you think? she says
I look around, the place
is a mess, there's something
on the table grown moldy
The floor's deep with socks,
underwear, magazines, newspapers
Well, it's small, I say, and
it's a mess, but I like it
I pose for her nude sometimes
says Pito, she followed me
home once, and she says
Take off your clothes, I want
to take your picture, and I say
take off your clothes first
and she does, so I do too
I'm really disappointed, I
say to Diane, I was really
hoping to introduce Pito

to someone new
So, says Diane, adjusting
one of her cameras, how about
if I take some pictures
Why don't you stand next
to Pito, she says, With our
clothes on? says Pito
Wait a minute, I say, this
isn't my idea of fun, I thought
we'd sit around drinking
some beers and talking
I open three beers from the
six-pack I brought but Diane
turns hers down, Come on
she says, you two, get closer
I'm getting nervous, Pito's
getting nervous, I walk to
the door, I'm leaving, I say
When I wake up from that dream
I call up Pito, Hey, I say
Remember all those dreams
you've been having of Diane
Arbus, I'm starting to have
them now, Pito grows quiet
on his end of the line
Finally he says, You go
to bed with her
Nawh, I say, I took her over
to meet you, but it turns out
you both already knew each other
And then she wanted to
take our photo together
And that's when I left

and I woke up and called you
That's good, says Pito
that you didn't go to bed
with her, otherwise
you woudn't be able
to get her out of your mind
I'm going crazy when I'm
awake, he says, I just
want to sleep and
dream about her, he says
You've gone to bed with
her? I ask, I think so
he says, but I'm not sure
When I wake up, I don't
remember that much
Just that I'm disappointed
to be waking up
She's something, isn't
she, I say, She's the
best, says Pito

Benjamin Sáenz

Resurrections

The stones themselves will sing.

Broken, Incan roads. The stones laid perfect
on mountains of snow so stubborn
not even blazing suns could beat it into water.
But the Incans could tame such mountains. With a fire
of their own, they knew how to melt that ice.
Stone by stone, step by step, the ancients
walked the highest path of earth. Stones,
tight knots that tied the world together. Roads, higher—
now stones are buried deep like bones
of Incan lords. Those roads, like Incan hands
who built them, refuse to lie still
in the ground. They loosen the wasted land.

▲

My mother lost him young, her older brother. She gave
my brother his name "because the moment he was born
his name rose on my lips." Ricardo, "A friend
took a stone, and broke his skull wide open—
and broke my mother's heart." She walks with him
on a path they took to school. There, in the sun, he laughs
until she wakes. Been forty years,
and grief is glued to her. Anger rises
in her voice: "But *here*," she grabs his picture,
Here he is perfect. *Here* he is not broken."

▲

The beer I drink is good tonight,
almost sweet, but cold. The dead are close.
Calm, I sit, touch the photographs of those
I walked with. Grandparents, uncles, not one
generation was spared. A brother. A niece.
In the country of their final exile
their legs will not cross the border.
Their feet will not touch my earth again
but tonight I hear their steps. I swallow,
must finish the beer I started. *Take this
all of you and drink. This is my blood.* Tired,
I drink from the cup, take the cold, within me now,
and wrap myself in faces of the dead:
stones which form a path where I walk still.

▲

The Mimbres buried their dead beneath their homes.
At night, softly, the buried
rose, re-entered the rooms of the living
as blankets woven with the heavy threads of memory,
blankets on which the Mimbres rested,
on which they slept, and dreamed.

Easter

My mother woke us that Sunday—her voice
a bell proclaiming spring. We rose
diving into our clothes, newly bought.
We took turns standing before mirrors,
combing, staring at our new selves.
Sinless from forty days of desert,

sinless from good confessions, we
drove to church in a red pickup, bright
and red and waxed for the special
occasion. Clean, polished as apples,
the yellow-dressed girls in front
with Mom and Dad; the boys in back,
our hair blowing free in the warming
wind. Winter gone away. At Mass,
the choir singing loud: ragged
noted from ragged angel's voices;
ancient hymns sung in crooked Latin.
The priest, white robed, raised his palms
toward God, opened his mouth in awe:
"Alleluia!" The unspoken word of Lent
let loose in flight. Alleluia and incense
rising, my mother wiping her tears
from words she'd heard; my brother and I
whispering names of statues lining
the walls of the church. Bells ringing,
Mass ending, we running to the truck,
shiny as shoes going dancing. Dad
driving us to see my grandmother. There,
at her house, I asked about the new word
I'd heard: *resurrection*. "Death,
death," she said, her hands moving downward,
"the cross—that is death." And then she
laughed: "The dead will rise." Her upturned
palms moved skyward as she spoke. "The dead
will rise." She moved her hands toward me,
wrapped my face with touches, and
laughed again. *The dead will rise.*

At Thirteen

At thirteen, I knew what it was to sin,
Knew what it was to love, to love the sin:
My curious hand reached down to touch
What was mine alone, rubbing

Clenching, grabbing, mesmerized
By a growing greed, something of men
Already in me, hard, harder, up and down,
Until my boyhood frenzy left me bathed

In sweat. The wet of discovery flooding
My stomach and chest, a milky rain
Of warmth from clouds within. That smell:
Moist morning cotton rose to my head.

I had to taste—so bitter awful, salty
As blood. I stretched across the bed, tired
Unable to return to my former sleep.
For a week, I could not face my father

Nor my mother, afraid that their eyes
Knew and accused. And Saturday, I ran
To church vomiting *O my God, I am heartily*
Sorry for having offended thee, and I detest

All my sins . . . My secret spilled
To forgiving priest, my voice trembling
Repentence in every word. I could have
Hid forever in dark shame. And after

healing words, newness and light. Innocent
Once more. I knelt, cried, prayed. Clean
And free, I went home, waited a week, then
Did it again and again—in awe of the miracle.

Creation. Trinity Site, New Mexico.
5:30 A.M., July 16th, 1945

Let there be light.
And there was light.

The sun was slow in arriving that morning
though it was no longer dark, was light enough,
and having been born with good eyes, we could see.
Motionless, we stood with a patience we rarely
practiced. Motionless, we stood on the cool,
cactus sand which was an ocean. It was hard
to imagine so much water in this place
of permanent thirst. Motionless, we stood
just as we once waited for our sons to struggle
out of our wives. The labor wasn't long,
but the longest ten seconds of our lives. Ten
seconds, that was all—
        And then the man-made flash—
twice as large as the sun—photographed the moment
in fire. Flames burning morning sands,
slashing the face of the calm.
        The ball of thunder strangled
the sky. Reached, blasted, bounced on rocks,
became a perfect tower—taller, wider, whiter
than the Aztecs ever dreamed or desired.

All the gilded temples where we crossed ourselves
and worshipped perished in the smoke. Everything
surpassed in the new incense. Falling.
On our knees, it seemed to reach for us.
We prayed for it to stop, yet urged it on.
The air exploded hot, grew cold, then hot again
invoking Indian winds to rise, to blow,
to break the earth in half.
   Then it was silent.
Motionless, we stood—the air throwing us
back, and we remembered our selves, our past,
the boyhood houses filled with women's singing.
We rose, surveyed the aftermath of our great
experiment. There was not much damage:
rearranged sand, uprooted bushes, a few dead
rabbits. This was, after all, already a desert,
already named *Jornada del Muerto*, plain
of the no personed God.
   We had seen. And lived.
We blessed ourselves, smelling the victory.
We put on jubilant smiles in the face
of the outcome. But the smiles fell off
unable to withstand the great success.
   The sun was slow in arriving that morning.
Those of us who bore witness saw it rise
in the new sky, motionless, but it no longer
gave enough light. Now, after many years,
our eyes have grown accustomed to the dark.

Luis Omar Salinas

Late Evening Conversation with My Friend's Dog, Moses, After Watching Visconti's The Innocent

Moses, who is there to save us
from the crickets, those small gods
in armor, nagging some vague truths
transient as Visconti's light
through the arbors of grapes and lilac?
I think the loquats have been sleeping
like our guardian angels and
who is to say what the moon is thinking?
Or the lost fragments of our hearts?
It could all be the end of air
in liquor, rain, or self-indulgence.
You could complain about each leaf
of the apricot, falling. I too
could catalog each woman that failed
to save me, and we both could be
as melancholy as clouds. Moses,
there are no prophecies in the sky,
only this earth, its gray at our
fingertips. Let's stop bitching
about death and the light of the lovers
on the veranda next door. I want
to explain, as you should too, about
the meekness of all the nights that
have passed, burnt-out stars or storms.
We must take control of the air
and breathe as only we can

like the icy throat of comets.
Listen to me Moses, we're not
as Biblical as rain, but our transgressions
go to the sea in search of speech.
Salt or otherwise, blood or otherwise,
things remain the same as long as we watch
the fiddles turn. And despite the women,
the rise and fall of French cinema,
the heart must dance like lightning,
burn, and save itself.

Crazy Gypsy

1.
I am Omar
   the crazy gypsy
      nimble footed
      and carefree

      I write poems
         on walls
            that crumble
            and fall

      I talk to shadows
         that sleep
            and go away
               crying

      I meet fearless girls
         who tell me

their troubles
my loneliness
bottled up in their
tummy.

2.
I am Omar
the crazy gypsy
I write songs
to my dead mother
hurl stones
at fat policemen
and walk on seaweed
in my dreams

I walk away from despair
like a horse walks away
from his master
end up in jail
eating powdered eggs
for breakfast

3.
My spine shakes
to the songs
of women

I am heartless and lonely
and I whistle a tune
out of one of my dreams
where the world
babbles out loud
and Mexican hatcheck girls

do the Salinas shuffle
a dance composed
by me in one
of my nightmares
and sold
for a bottle
of tequila

4.
I am Omar
the crazy gypsy
I waltz through avenues
of roses
to the song
of Mariachis

5.
I am Omar
the Mexican gypsy
I speak of love
as something whimsical and aloof
as something naked and cruel
I speak of death
as something inhabiting
the sea
awkward and removed

I speak of hate
as something nibbling my ear.

This Is About the Way It Should Be

I listen to the frantic philosophy
of swallows on forgotten Tuesdays
at our reunion where everyone
appears to be drunk, idly
moved with indifference,
or sadly scratching.
I am then reminded
of my poor manners,
posthumous remarks on literature
and the avant-garde.
I am told repeatedly
that I am crazy, that I make
a poor husband, and that
I will end in a bad death.

I will all this to Seville,
Toledo, my home state
and all the illegitimate
children I wish I'd had.
I give all this to the Politico
who eulogized my name
without knowing I was still
alive and writing.
And last of all I give
this poor rendering
of my emotional state
to a woman who wants
everything, even my shoes.

In Mazatlán

after a vision of Shelley being cremated on the Mexican coast

Being a bachelor is crazy business,
    in Mazatlán I thought I was the Mexican
      Shelley. And casting glances
           at the Primavera seagulls
        I lost myself there—
           like a deep afternoon sky.
I left my heart
    standing among the people
      in their revolution
           of joy
        and dog-beaten
        saludos.
My bones singing to Shelley
           in his awful voyage
      as the Mayan Gods
           spears in hand
watch from a distance,
      and I cavort
           among the maidens.
I take myself there
        a visionary
among tales of fortune
    and disillusionment.
And toss my soul
    like a madman
        tying to emulate
          scholarly diction,
and flounder

in the waves,
ghost in the horizon.
I toss these festered arms
    into political blunders
    and poetic anarchy
professing a kinship
    with the sea.
This bachelor of little eloquence
    has a fate to surrender to
        and in the quiet whispers
        of morning
        walks with legendary
        poetic heroes,
watching the sun rise
    like a mother.
It takes a fool to be a poet;
    an evil wonder lies at bay,
    good-bye Mazatlán,
        you have surrendered to me
        like a woman,
throwing her blouse into the sea.

I'm Walking Behind the Spanish

eavesdropping on their conversation:
Neruda sound asleep.
Juan Ramón placing yellow flowers
in his kitchen.
Miguel in jail.
Lorca playing flamenco
to a house full of romanceros.

César Vallejo walking through
the streets of Paris.
I walk behind you
carrying this heart
of white rain which has
come out of the barrio
with the turbulence of
the Guadalquivir.
The sun is a witness
to your coming and going
like soldiers marching
towards the sea.
And this petty inquisitive
brain has watched you
enter my life.
Miguel weeping.
Lorca clean shaven and alert
murdered standing.
Neruda calm like dropping fruit.
Juan Ramón Jiménez
in a portrait of yellow flowers.
And Vallejo drunk with the ghost
of compassion, sipping cold coffee.

▲

Behind time I'm
like a lost finger
in the sea.
Thrashing about
looking for a lost heaven.
I go dizzy through the crowds
whispering a tender
folktale as if to a ghost.

I'm taking everything
to the sea, toss bird bones
there, eat bread and hold on.

▲

I'm walking behind
the Spanish in a Madrigal
dream.
The Cow lays down,
the worker goes home
to his wife of complaints.
The banker can't spend
his money.

▲

I lead a tragic life
but I have the optimism of
the owl.
Forlorn diplomat
of my existence
I go in soldier fashion
through life—
scarred, foolish
and romantic.
Making the best
of what is there.
And feel the tug
of angels in my footsteps.

I Am America

It's a hell of a world.
I go like a schoolboy stepping
through the murderous countryside,
a bit of rhyme, a little drunk
with the wonderful juices of breasts,
and the magnificent
with their magicianlike words
slipping into the voice of America.
I carry my father's coat,
some coins,
my childhood eyes in wonder—
the olive trucks plucky
in their brash ride
through the avenue,
the wino in a halo of freedom,
the shopkeepers of democracy.

I am brave, I am sad
and I am happy with the workers in the field,
the pregnant women
in ten dollar dresses,
the night air supping
and stopping to chat
like a wild romantic lady.
Children's voices and dogs,
the bar, the songs and fights.
I go ruminating in the brothels,
the ghettos, the jails.
Braggart, walking into early
cafés confessing the naïveté

and love for the unemployed.
I'm a dream in the land
like the Black, Mexican, Indian,
Anglo and Oriental faces
with their pictures of justice.
I go gaudy into movie houses,
flamboyant spectator
of horse faces.
I am not unloved, or unwanted
but I have seen the faces
of the rebel, the outcast,
I have touched the madness, all the terrible
and I have seen the ghosts of the past.
I am a friend to all,
for I have touched everything,
even the empty plates of the poor.
I put on my clothes, my hat,
I visit everywhere—
I go to market for bananas,
smoke the air,
breathe America.

I am wretched and mean,
I am kind and compassionate.
I remember catechism class,
the nuns and the priests,
my sister's wit,
and the neighbor's beautiful wife.
I am walking behind America,
suspicious, pie-eyed,
open-faced in the distance.
I am a father of prayers,
obedient,

I am a father of women,
a son of women.
I speak as the common man
and listen like the wise.
I am America,
and by hearts grown cold to me
I will be the seer of my intellect.
I will put an end to misery with
the bravado of the seeker,
drunken, reveling
in this American continent,
tightfisted,
exposed like a blue rose
to the night stars.

Gary Soto

The Seventieth Year

We hear you want to die.
What is it?
The hair on an arm
Leaning toward the shadows?

Sun-Maid is gone, Grandpa,
The machinery fleeced in rust.
Though the loading dock holds the years
Of rain, sweat that fell
And opened into momentary coins,
Work has stopped. You can sleep now.
Sunlight enters the house,
Dust drifts in a galaxy
Of unmapped motes. And Grandma?
She is well—her veins no longer
Surfacing under a blue flesh.
She's with you now
And her warmth is a nightly presence.
Get up and eat, Grandpa.
Your skin has yellowed.
Looked at the backyard garden—
Already the flower beds
Brim with summer weeds
And ants unravel
From their dark holes in the trees.
Come to the kitchen.
It is warm there, Grandpa,

And your family, the little ones
With their cards of Get Well,
Has gathered like a small cloud,
Like the steam weeping
On the window.

A Red Palm

You're in this dream of cotton plants.
You raise a hoe swing, and the first weeds
Fall with a sigh. You take another step,
Chop, and the sigh comes again,
Until you yourself are breathing that way
With each step, a sigh that will follow you into town.

That's hours later. The sun is a red blister
Coming up in your palm. Your back is strong,
Young, not yet the broken chair
In an abandoned school of dry spiders.
Dust settles on your forehead, dirt
Smiles under each fingernail.
You chop, step, and by the end of the first row,
You can buy one splendid fish for wife
And three sons. Ten hours and the cupboards creak.
You can rest in the backyard under a tree.
Your hands twitch on your lap,
Not unlike the fish on a pier or the bottom
of a boat. You drink iced tea. The minutes jerk
Like flies. It's dusk, now night,
And the lights in your home are on.
That costs money, yellow light

In the kitchen. That's thirty steps,
You say to your hands,
Now shaped into binoculars.
You could raise them to your eyes:
You were a fool in school, now look at you.
You're a giant among cotton plants,
The lung-shaped leaves that run breathing for miles.
Now you see your oldest boy, also running.
Papa, he says, it's time to come in,
You pull him into your lap
And ask, What's forty times nine?
He knows as well as you, and you smile.
The wind makes peace with the trees,
The stars strike themselves in the dark.
You get up and walk with a sigh of cotton plants.
You go to sleep with a red sun on your palm,
The sore light you see when you first stir in bed.

Pink Hands

I miss not eating fish on Friday,
The halved lemon squeezed a third time around,
And our prayers, silent mutters
To God, whom we knew, whom we trusted
To make things right. I miss the incense,
White scarf of smoke, and Monsignor Singleton
Saying mass in Latin, with his back to us.
When he raised the host, I looked down,
Usually at my hands, which were pink like the underside
Of a starfish. I miss the nuns, and the chalk smells
Of popped erasers, and the peppery corduroy

That swished when we walked. I never understood
The trinity, and still have doubts,
But was happy for the Father, Son, and Holy Ghost.
I miss Sister María, her white dove skin,
And the pagan babies waiting for our candles.
My favorite country was the boot country—Italy.
The Pope lived there, in his many robes,
And one of its cities was all canal.
This made me dream a lot. I wished my town
Were water, not dry lawns and thirsty kids.
I also like France, which was Catholic,
And England, which was not Catholic
But green and cool like the insides of trees.
I miss walking home in my Catholic clothes.
I miss crossing myself when an ambulance raced its siren.
At home a crucifix hung in almost every room,
Holy water in the cupboard behind the jam
And a box of pretzels, and a Bible
We seldom opened. Palm-leaf crosses from
Last spring withered in the window
For our Okie neighbors to look at in awe.

Okies are now the homeless, car salesmen
and waitresses. The pagan babies are the simple poor,
The nuns in their sleds of black shadow,
Women with skirts up to their knees.
Our school, condemned by the city, now creaks
With mice, not the polished shoes of Catholicism.
In school, I didn't mean to be bad.
I write I WILL NOT TALK BACK a lot of times
On the blackboard, and some of that dust
Worked into my soul. Now I'm quiet,
The telephone is quiet, my family

And the people I like best are quiet.
The nuns would be proud of me,
And so would Monsignor Singleton,
Who once begged me to please be quiet in the confessional.
But Monsignor, I can't help talking.
The Church is changed. We have folksy guitars
And an electric bass to thump our hearts, croissants
Instead of donuts, and three kinds of coffee,
Juice if you want. There are more lawyers
Than ever, doctors, teachers, and educated people
Looking for a way out. There are retreats,
Young Adult groups, spaghetti dinners
For parents without partners,
Five-mile runs for priests and nuns,
Lay ministry, fewer bingo nights, more poor people
Cuddling newspapers over warm grates of steam.
Monsignor, good priest who stared holiness
Into my body, the church on Pine is in trouble:
At the altar of Mary, we have electric lights,
Not candles, sitting in the votive cups.
You drop a quarter
Into a slot and a single bulb comes on.
Two or three more quarters, more sins
Notching the soul, and the whole
Altar is a pinball machine. How do we kneel
And pray at such a place? Monsignor, come back,
With a holy slight of hand, with the smoke,
The wavering flame, the glow of the votive cup
Like a red taillight, the teary melt
of wax.

Who Will Know Us?

for Jaroslav Siefert

It is cold, bitter as a penny.
I'm on a train, rocking toward the cemetery
To visit the dead who now
Breathe through the grass, through me,
Through relatives who will come
And ask, Where are you?
Cold. The train with its cargo
Of icy coal, the conductor
With his loose buttons like heads of crucified saints,
His mad puncher biting zeros through tickets.

The window that looks onto its slate of old snow.
Cows. The barbed fences throat-deep in white.
Farmhouses dark, one wagon
With a shivering horse.
This is my country, white with no words,
House of silence, horse that won't budge
To cast a new shadow. Fence posts
That are the people, spotted cows the machinery
That feeds officials. I have nothing
Good to say. I love Paris
And write, "Long Live Paris!"
I love Athens and write,
"The great book is still in her lap."
Bats have intrigued me,
The pink vein in a lilac.
I've longed to open an umbrella
In an English rain, smoke

And not give myself away,
Drink and call a friend across the room,
Stomp my feet at the smallest joke.
But this is my country.
I walk a lot, sleep.
I eat in my room, read in my room,
And make up women in my head—
Nostalgia that's the cigarette lighter from before the war,
Beauty that's tears that flow inward to feel its roots.

The train. Red coal of evil.
We're its passengers, the old and young alike.
Who will know us when we breathe through the grass?

Carmen Tafolla

Hot Line

to my firstborn, firstdead, para mi'ija.

The mark of you is soft and bright on my body
    The ridge is smooth up my belly
        disrupted even
        deep and rich in color
                and unforgettable

                like you.

The feel of it against my curious fingers
      is not like skin
      but different—
          like promises and memories
          and passionate peace in one.

The scar is somehow like concentrated satin—
        a yard of it per half centimeter—
        rare, distinct, and full of voice and story
        (The aged *viejita* that I'd met
        so long ago had said
             "Each thing upon this earth
             has *voz, virtud, e idioma*—
        voice and use and language.")

This mark of you on me
                        is full
                        of language

                        and
                        of
                        love.

It is your gift to me.
Each night I can reach down and feel it,
listen,
hear your message

on this our own
                        private

                        red

                        hot line.

La Miss Low

La Miss Low
was tall and thin
and wore her pale hair tight
on her small head
like the skin
of a pea.
La Rosary always said
she wished she could comb her
well

so she would look
pretty
but since she was a teacher
and were just kids,
La Rosary told her
nothing.

La Miss Low would stand close
to Mr. Mason
thinking, we think,
to appear more elegant
by standing in close proximity
to a man,
even if he was married
and with a crewcut that only he
thought made him look handsome,
but when he turned his head
to her
to say a few words,
between classes, in that noisy hall,
it was just them,
the two of them,
Hero and Heroine,
amidst all of us kids,
and she felt
mature,
elegant,
intimate,
laughing slow and sophisticated
at anything
he said.

La Miss Low didn't say much
tried to raise her head high
like a noble figure,
to let her silence
(guardian of the princess)
speak for her,
speak complex things,
very sensitive things,
to keep her face without expression,
thereby showing the nobility of her soul,
to set a superior example
for these uncultured children.

La Rosary would say
that if she could comb her hair for her,
full and soft,
and let it grow
a little,
and add a few curls . . .
if she could paint that face
with a bit more color
and teach her to let go a little,
to let her feelings show,
that she could make her
look
prettier.

La Miss Low
was tall and thin
and posed herself
like a statue
of civilization
amidst chaos

while La Rosary saw her
like fertile ground, awaiting the seed,
and Rosary there, wanting to cultivate,
willingly, her garden.
"Did you get number 7?" I would ask her,
and she would open her book with a long sigh,
saying, "I could make her
look
real pretty."
But since she was a teacher
and we were just kids,
La Rosary
told her nothing.

Poquito Allá

"This hand?"
"This hand?" he says,
"It was an accident.
You do not understand—
poquito aquí, poquito allá—
that's how *Dios* meant it, *ves*, to be.
It doesn't bother me too much
In fact," he laughs, "It gives me less to work about.
Less people who will trust their broken chairs to me.
Yet I can still these roses plant,
like that one, standing by your feet—
'*Las Siete Hermanas*,' for they always bloom together,
like sweet sisters—seven in each bunch.
And I can still make chocolate, stirring strong,

the fingers do not slow me down—
these two, nor this one sewed back on.

"It's funny, don't you think,
how in those many years at Kelly Field
or even in the war, *Dios sólo sabe*, so many
around me dead, or legs or arms just floating off to sea—
but I came back (it must have been my mother's prayers)
the only thing the worse for it my teeth
(the Navy took us perfect, sent us back a mess)
and yet—
I had so much—
aun every limb and digit there
my whole life full,
and so I can't complain
this hand still does so much
for me—why just today
I planted ten small seeds—
cilantro for Mama
(that woman loves it even in her beans)
and pressed the earth down on them soft,
like her soft fingers when she caresses me,
and picked the eggs out for my sisters
y sus nietos—they taste different fresh,
like this, *las tiendas no comparan*—

"But you want to know what happened?
Well, it's not too bad, *nomás que*
Chuy's neighbor still won't talk to me,
goes way around the grocery store
when he runs into me
I guess he's scared to see.
Los gringos, sometimes, *son así*.

Se siente mal, because he was the one who said
Reach down in there and get that wrench
and then he flipped the switch too soon—
ya casi era tiempo de salir—
I'd work for him all day and he
was eager to pay up, clean up, go home,
and didn't wait to see that it was out.
Así—se acabó.
The doctors sewed this one back on,
aunque los que no están
molestan menos que éste aquí.

"Too bad it bothers him so much.
I still do all I used to 'cept for
playing the guitar and carving wood.
The rest I do jus fine, tho's maybe not as good.
Y *el pobre* always was uncomfortable with Mexicans—
y ahora peor.
Forgot to pay me for that day
or maybe scared to send the cash
for fear I'd ask for more.
Well that's OK—this hand
still knows to *saludar,* shake hands, *y abrazar*
and only yesterday, my baby grandson stood right up,
solito, holding on to these good fingers
here.
Derecho, fuerte, unafraid.
Poquito aquí, poquito allá."

Ernesto Trejo

The Cloud Unfolding

It starts with the picture of my grandfather,
machine gunned in his car, Packard De Luxe, 1923.
A snapshot with poor composition, slightly
out of focus, it holds the forty-three
bullets that pushed for light or air
& which now find their black spaces and obey
our eyes. His last curse will never leave
this picture, his body will never
leave that car, his blood will forever
cake on the red upholstery
(someone pulled you out of the car, someone else
unfolded a blanket over your face not knowing
that you wanted to see that cloud unfold
over the whole sky
or gather into rain & flood your eyes.
Your last curse gave way to visions of battle,
of other men, never yourself,
dying in the heat & the dust).
In El Paso my grandfather once stayed up
all night & when the sun rose he shaved the goatee,
tapped over his heart & felt the fake passport.
Later he emerged from the hotel a businessman,
like Lenis, & walked six blocks to the train station,
a black mushroom in the fog,
a piece of shit under the sky of El Paso
or Geneva, a sky that ate his shirts & sucked
his head into a chisel of anger.

Further back, in one autumn the Eiffel went up,
a symbol of itself, & every washerwoman
felt proud of her city
(But one night, in 1936, the tower would crack,
collapsing over Los Angeles, against the pavement
dressed with spit & yellow newspapers
that told the Negros Burn, *Generation of Vipers*
& the Mexicans *Go Back Where You Came From.*
Roosevelt, the syphilitic Jew, will sell
to the Germans tomorrow at 10:15. My father
is in his kitchen, dropping ice cubes in a glass
of water, when the phone rings & a man
tells him that his bar is in flames.
When my father arrives at the bar, nine years
of good luck go up in smoke & someone tells him
it was the Negroes, your brother refused them credit.
My father nods, not knowing why, & stands
there for hours following the slow cloud from his bar
until the sun silhouettes the church two blocks away
& he thinks *that shadow is a bad omen*).
Father, for the rest of your life, in Mexico,
you never mentioned the fire
but spoke of flappers, of Roosevelt, of Chaplin
devoured by a clock on his way to work.

Cipriana

my grandmother, in memoriam

1.
There were trains that went in the tunnels
and never came out. The eyes of horses
focused and trotted to their deaths.
The corn slept in the cistern
and was rotted when it woke.

2.
An old photo. You are next to your marigolds
(the flower of death, mother tells me)
and I cling to your skirt. How strange to be four,
watching the print on your skirt. Behind us
the paint peeled off the wall all morning,
your honeysuckle thirsted for light, your ivy
found a crevice and went in.

3.
You never saw the sea or the pelicans
winged like angels. In the end, your visions
were embarrassing: a granddaughter
sleeping with Satan; a voice in every corner,
beckoning; your husband, the blind man
lost in prayer, a daddy that would punish.
Your daughters, aging, won't talk about the end.
I do. I take the space in which you lived,
your life, and put it in my pocket, and name you.

The President Is Up Before the Fruit Vendor

The president is up before the fruit vendor
and goes to bed after the bus driver.
He says: history is unfair.
If the president has a toothache, we grieve.
If he smiles, we smile.
Sometimes we think we like him and we sleep
happy for it. But once we are asleep
it's different. He worries
and makes laws about our dreams.
We may not dream in other languages.
We may not dream about a life without him.
We may not dream if he's out of the country.
But there are ways . . .
We dream while we work and while we eat.
When we smile at him and shake his hand,
we're dreaming. Sometimes we see his picture
and dream of his glasses streaked with blood,
his chin tunneled by worms. Around the mouth
that punishes and forgives a string of flies
silences what could be a last word. Below,
his chest is covered with the spit of children.
Since we have never seen his eyes
we don't dream about them; they are windows
that send their black light into our hearts.

For Jaime Sabines

Even God has called it a day.
The streets of Tuxtla are empty
like the bottles of white rum
after the party.
Crickets hum discreetly.
It is so quiet.
When the dead come out
and hush secrets in the ears of young girls
their nightgowns rustle toward the fields
where oxen stumble among the high grasses.

Maybe tonight some peasants have met death
in their sleep.
Maybe their bodies will be offered
to the vultures tomorrow
and it won't matter,
for in this country no one is sure
of anything.
In this country it is best to get drunk
and forget.

And you are almost drunk,
almost sure that your hands sprouted moles,
and think of your brother and the dark
river of blood between you.

But these things don't exist
in your poems.

Who said life would be easy?
Put out your cigarette.
Drench yourself in the hot, moist night,
like a star, adrift and hopeless.

Robert Vasquez

Early Morning Test Light over Nevada, 1955

Your mother slept through it all,
her face turned away
like the dark side of the earth.

We'd heard
between *rancheras* on the radio
that the ladles
and the two bears
that lie among the stars
above Nevada
would fade at 3:15 as though seared
by a false sun.

The stove exhaled all night
a trinity of blue rings. You entered
your fourth month
of floating in the tropical,
star-crossed water
your mother carried under her heart
that opens and closes
like a butterfly.

When the sky flared,
our room lit up. Cobwebs
sparkled on the walls, and a spider
absorbed the light
like a chameleon and began

to inch toward the outer rings
as if a fly trembled.

Roosters crowed. The dog
scratched at the door. I went outside
hearing the hens and thought *weasel*
and found broken eggs, the chicks
spongy, their eyes
stunned and shrouded
by thin veils of skin.

"Don't open your eyes,"
I whispered to you when darkness
returned. I thought of your bones
still a white gel, I remembered the story
of blood smeared on doorways,
and I placed my hand on the balloon
you rode that would slowly sink
to your birth. I said
the Old German name your mother already picked
for you, *Robert*. It means *bright fame*.

Día de los Muertos

for Lowry

November, zinnias late
and lifting toward nightshade.
A boy I know plays dead,
unaware of the blood-orange
nimbuses that sweep by, heaven

withheld from a face
partial to rain and squalls
of color at sunset. When porchlights
turn mothy, his father
will whistle him in, this kid
who can shake off death
like so much grit and grass
at evening's end. Houselights
will blink out, and mothers
will take fathers to bed,
and a child nuzzling sleep
will hear cries
which might be the groans
of the dying or the groans
of love. . . .

       And I'm the neighbor
gone loveless for years
and walled off by eucalyptus
and brick. I'm the silent one
drawn to bonfires, those
in alleyways and in the sky,
who finger-traces the flamelights
that blue and smoke out, leaf
upon leaf, star upon star.
I must become flame-like to go
beyond bucktoothed fences
and horse stalls and a horse's neigh;
I must inchworm my way
up a cindery path, believing
the Dog Star will yield
its back and ferry me across
the blue-black fathoms.

I'd like to think
that heaven's long acres
are scored with roses, island roses
belled open by the bees
with their true appetite
for all orders that bloom.

California Sonnets: Night Sequence

for Mary Ann, & for the doctor

1.

I look up at the night's broad back
gone crazy with tattoos of light, seasonal
signs almost beyond stoppage, and let
the unsayable build skyward. As it is
I've put off sleep, its gray tunnel
circular and face-filled, to take in blue
pulse-points that work the peninsular dark.
Last night, below the ridgeline that blocks
out the ocean's amplitude, a woman
called me to bed. And slow's the sprawl
of the almost-in-love, their wave and blur
charging their own amplitude. Yielding, we took
to the windowsill, like children almost, the curtains
blown wide as if calling the star-sprawl in, almost.

2.

Witness the Bear's stoked belly, his burning
stupor commanding the rooftops . . . Of course
this changes nothing; by morning the windows

are wing-sliced; all day the languid ladies
of the field and wild cowpeas still carry
hillsides into spring; the live oak's true
posture of pain deepens. But I know,
due to celestial warp, some stars are black
cinders where they seem to blaze: scars
of light that survive the body. Dead suns
do that; they haunt with their ghost-lit patinas;
they reach us with their fixed and mapped
movements, like old lovers: pliable arcs of light,
they come on inarticulate, glassy, and sure.

3.
For the nightsky's vault issues insomnia,
someone said, those troubled hours withholding
the passage and balance good sleep drifts back to.
In Los Altos I join the bare-knuckled ones
who browse the neoprene bags and dumpster spillage.
And my nose swells with the road-smear of skunk, not
the living kind that will not scare, but a tire-
smashed stripe, creamy clear, almost afloat.
They say eternity's a channel in the sky.
—As if the skunk soul veers upward and drafts
like a kite.—As if the skunk angels
could spot this small jaywalker, stalled
like the number 1, beneath the intersections
of heaven.—As if I were in love.

4.
Out of the fissured earth, columbine will mount,
suffer, and sustain acres of thistle and mud;
the high, plain shouts of children
half-heard a block away at recess will strive

to twine the day together. Bells and mission. But
before you rise from sleep's wash, think of raccoons
arrogant on Dixon Way, who palm chicken bones
before they rehouse the flood drains; think
of me hogging a whole street the way ladles
hog zones in the sky. Think how the wintered
and rolling earth reveals itself, how
everything the night holds out and clarifies,
like love, withdraws suddenly from the limbs
and organs of intake: hands, eyes, and heart.

Coyotes

I've bicycled out
into the blue fieldlight
to glimpse them: a few flecks
zigzagging down a hillside,
drawn to the lighted compounds

igniting at this hour
and echoing the sky. Before long
they stop, shy of a smell
or barbed wire, circling
on old pissed-on ground

yellowed once more, and wait.
Once, as a child in a field
flush with poppies, I found
a carcass, split open
and shelled of all gray

sponge-like organs, the heart
and lungs gone from this vest
of coyote, the head
still intact, the jaws
squinched upward and open.

That night, in a dream
or awake, I heard the canine
dark flourish, unchecked
like wisteria, climbing
nightlong into my room. "Awful,"

one could say, like frayed notes
from the trumpet I would soon
give up, the brass valves—"Three
throats," my teacher once said—
suffering all that spit. "It's all

just vibrations in the air,"
Mr. Sessions would say, half
joking and half in awe when we
were all in tune. But out there
I imagined the splayed

pelt was shuddering, gathering
the field's orange swirl and sway
blowing into it, the troubled
snout fluent once more and firing
its off-key aria that singes

the dark. Now I lie
between thistle and buttercups,
belly down and thick
with childhood's prolonged pain,
and under the clear polish

of moonlight I watch three
long skulls tilt back
as if they could sing
down the moon: a remnant bone
summoned back and willing to rise.

Alma Luz Villanueva

The Balance

"I've told you that the true art of a warrior is to balance terror and wonder."
—DON JUAN

The mark of Merlin
Hawk is on my window—
its clear substance that
looks like a bird
in flight. Stunned,

I picked you up, wings
stilled, black talons
dug into my hand, your
fierce love—you
look at me with one
red eye, burning.

I held you, hawk.

You speak to me of
nothing less than life—
nothing less than death—
nothing less than this
will do. I

placed you on a tree
stump, to make your
choice. My son said,

"What isn't balanced,
in nature, must
die." "Sometimes
that balance must be
found," I say.

I held you with love,

in my hands, with
a terror and a wonder.

Wolf at the Door

1.
The wolf slipped into the supermarket—
someone muttered, "Goddamn dog,
people should take care their goddamned
dogs." The wolf's paws

scratched the shiny floors, her
nose twitched nervously and the
lights blinded her. There were no
smells, no wind, no sun; there

were people looking hungrily
from side to side. The wolf
climbed up on a shelf and got videoed
by a camera. All she smelled was

boredom and fear. She was no longer
curious, not even a mouse. The wolf
stuck her muzzle up and howled. Then,
she disappeared.

2.
The wolf upon seeing a collar on
the dog, refused to enter the dog's
house and be fed, so, supposedly,
she starved: you know, I don't

believe this. I mean, maybe she
was shot and skinned and made
into a fur coat: but I know
a wolf can always hunt.

You see the woman with the wild
hair smelling apples just to see
if they're real, the way she squeezes
the hamburger and shakes the milk

around, just to see if they're real.
You see, the woman is the wolf
with the power to open doors.
She scowls at the camera's eye.

3.
She will go home and make tacos,
pick up a photo magazine and read
about a German camp survivor
who supervised 2,000 children

made to carry small stones, who
were fed soup with bits of potatoes
and human flesh. This is when
the woman puts her muzzle skyward

and howls like a wolf. This is when
there's no camera, no witness, and she
is thankful she's part animal, so the
terrible burden of her humanness

will not crush her soul.
This is when she lets
the wolf in: the wolf who
waits at the door.

Things of Our Childhood

to Marc, in his twenty-first year

I watch you defy your death,
climbing the sheer mountain cliff
until you become a dot.
I do not say, "Come back,
you'll kill yourself!" No, I stopped
that a while ago, and I watch you
climb with joy, as I climb with joy;

so I understand, only you go straight up
and I go sideways, then up—but I get
there. We talk and the lake listens,
then the fire, and finally, just the

stars. The first night we sat on granite
as galaxies appeared in the dark, cold
lake; I told you things of my childhood,
and, later, things of your childhood.
I lead, you lead. Mother, son.
Man and woman. Backpacking out,

you go ahead; I stop often, touching
trees, stones, whispering my goodbyes,
knowing there are no goodbyes. Knowing
you will greet me. Soon.

Power

You come from a line of
healing women: *doctoras, brujas.*

Doctors, sorceress. Though, actually,
in the Spanish dictionary, *brujo* is

sorcerer, conjurer, wizard—while
bruja is witch, hag, owl. Ha!

Then owl it shall be. Your great-
grandmother was an owl; your great-

great-grandmother was an owl,
and your mother is a witch,

a hag, and an owl. Witch and hag
has always—in time, only 5,000 years

before that Her magic and
Her beauty shone—meant a woman with

power; your great-great-grand
mother, Isidra, traveled Sonora

healing, and she married five
times, each time a better man;

your great-grandmother, Jesus, married
to a man of God, healed from wild

weeds and flowers picked from
vacant lots in Los Angeles.

Your grandmother, Lydia, heard
the healing music through her finger-

tips, but the music burned her:
witch, hag, witch. And I, your

mother, hear the word, healing
me, you, us, and though I burn,

I fly, too: owl, hawk, raven, my
eagle. Hummingbird, sparrow, jay,

mockingbird, snow owl, barn owl,
great-horned owl, pelican, golden

eagle. So, daughter, healer, take my
name: be a witch, a hag, a sorceress.

Take your power and fly like all
the women before you.

Fly Antoinetta Theresa
Villanueva.

Tino Villanueva

On the Subject of Staying Whole

With orange soda and scoops of popcorn,
I have taken the vague wisdom of the
Body to my favorite last row seat at the
Movie house. It is 1956 . . . and Sarge,
Keeper of the Lone Star house, Sarge,

Always Sarge, facing down everything
From the screen. I am fourteen and the
Muscles come to a stop: From the spell
Of too much make-believe world that is
Real. If I yell, "Nooooo!, nooooo!,"

Would the projectionist stop the last
Reel of the machine? Would the audience
Rise up with me to rip down the screen?
I think now how it went: nothing was

Coming out of me that could choke off
The sentences of Sarge, a world-beater
Released into history I would later turn
Against. A second-skin had come over me

In a shimmer of color and light. I could
Not break free from the event that began
To inhabit me—gone was the way to dream

Outside myself. From inside, a small
Fire began to burn like deep doubt or

A world fallen . . . I held on. I held on.

The Trailing Consequence: A Triptych

1.
Journey Home

The picture show, three-and-a-half hours of it,
was over;
the credits, so many,
ascended into immortality,

The fiery art of film
had sent my head buzzing—:
I arose in penumbra, vexed at the unwinding
course of truth and was now lost in my steps,
eyes struggling with unnatural chasms of light.
I walked home for a long time
and in my mind   I regarded
the tall screen bearing down on me—
I was drifting away
from its outburst, yet its measure of violence,
like an indictment from Sarge,
did not fade.

There was no wind.
No firm star came out
to acquire me in safety.

The world seemed enormous around me
and as I moved in it
I felt I could not journey
further than myself.

Minutes passed
and then another.
(Once I saw, as in a dream,
that I had never reached home.)
I crossed the railroad tracks, went past
the lumber yard, the concrete bridge at Purgatory Creek,
and over a second set of tracks—
a weary logic leading me back to where I began.
I think I must have made a fist
in desperation, as tough as the years
to my name
and there grew in my mouth
a great shout which never came.

Time and time over: a child at that age
falls short of endowing dumb misery with speech.

2.
Observer and Observed

No one walks with me
(down the dust-bound street
where I step lightly),
sullen, slight-young boy.
Each neighbor,
in the ease of the afternoon
serenely grown out of something forgetful,
looks through me,

believing life goes on as before
as I pass by.
The trees and the houses among them
see me staring in muteness;
from where they stand—houses, trees,
neighbors—they cannot know
the sudden intake of all breath,
a sigh I myself do not comprehend.

Something weightless
gathers around me, while my body, unpoised,
holds it forward momentum
in silence and slow time.

As the afternoon   emptied of meaning

deepens perceptively,

the soft-hollowed steps in which I move
are my only cause.

3.
Dusk with Dreaming

The neighborhood, 1956:
I reached its border
feeling I was nothing
other than my name.
It seems a long time ago
that I stepped into the patio,
held off for a moment
before going in for supper
and leaned, instead,

against a pecan tree's
slender-rooted trunk.
And standing in childhood, at my point of view,
I felt a nothingness
burning through all thought.

By now the day was fading into twilight,
and I beginning
not to cast a shadow where I had always been,
when I saw,
suddenly, a boy alone
who had to tear to prove he was . . .
Something from the movie screen had
dropped into life, his small shield of faith
no longer with him.

Dusk was dawning over the treetops
when I was called inside
where grace was said, I am sure of it,
for we were always grateful to the sky.
I remember the clock ticking

and my breathing

when finally

my mouth took ethnically again
sustenance in solace.
The rest of me began to dream and my mind
flew off and I became, for that instant:

another boy from another land, in another time,
another time, which is also home.

Biographical Notes

FRANCISCO ALARCÓN is the author of several books of poetry, including *The Earthquake Poems* (Humanizarte Publications), *Tattoos* (Humanizarte Publications), *Body in Flames/Cuerpo en Llamas*, and *Snake Poems* (both Chronicle Books). His work has been anthologized in various publications, including *Palabra Nueva: Cuentos Chicanos* and *Practicing Angels: Contemporary Anthology of San Francisco Bay Area Poetry*. He is a recipient of a 1989–90 Writer's Fellowship from the California Arts Council, a former Danforth and Fulbright Fellow, and is currently a professor at the University of California at Santa Cruz.

JIMMY SANTIAGO BACA is the author of three books of poetry, *Immigrants in Our Own Land and Selected Earlier Poems*, *Martín & Meditations on the South Valley*, and *The Black Mesa Poems*, all published by New Directions. He has received a fellowship from the National Endowment for the Arts, a 1988 Before Columbus Foundation American Book Award, and a 1989 International Hispanic Heritage Award. He lives in Albuquerque, New Mexico.

CORDELIA CANDELARIA is the author of two books of criticism, *Chicano Poetry: A Critical Introduction* and *Seeking the Perfect Game: Baseball in American Literature*, both published by Greenwood Press and a book of poetry, *Ojo de la Cueva/Cave Springs* (Maize Press). She teaches in the Chicano Studies Program at Arizona State University in Tempe.

ANA CASTILLO is the author of two novels, including *Sapogonia* (Bilingual Review Press) and a book of poetry, *My Father Was a Toltec* (West End Press). She received a fellowship from the National Endowment for the Arts and an American Book Award in fiction from the Before Columbus Foundation. She lives in Albuquerque, New Mexico.

ROSEMARY CATACALOS is the author of a chapbook, *As Long as It Takes* (Iguana Press) and a full-length collection of poetry, *Again for the First Time* (Tooth of Time Press), for which she was awarded the Texas Institute of Letters Prize in Poetry. She is a former recipient of the Dobie Paisano Fellowship, directed the Literature Program at the Guadalupe Cultural Arts Center in San Antonio, Texas, and is presently the Director of the Poetry Center at San Francisco State University.

LORNA DEE CERVANTES is the editor of *Red Dirt*, a new magazine of multicultural literature. She is the author of two books of poetry, *Emplumada* (University of Pittsburgh Press) and *From the Cables of Genocide: Poems on Love and Hunger* (Arte Público Press). She teaches in the Creative Writing Program at the University of Colorado in Boulder.

LUCHA CORPI is a founding member of Aztlán Cultural/Centro Chicano de Escritores, a writer's organization and the author of two books of poetry, *Noon Words* (Fuego de Aztlán Press) and *Variations on a Storm* (Third Woman Press). Her novel, *Delia's Song*, was published by Arte Público Press in 1989. She teaches in the Neighborhood Centers Program in Oakland, California.

CARLOS CUMPIÁN is the editor and publisher of March/Abrazo Press and one of the most active literary organizers in the city of Chicago. His anthology of Chicano poets, *Emergency Tacos* (March/Abrazo Press) has received great critical acclaim. His book of poetry is *Coyote Sun* (March/Abrazo Press).

ANGELA DE HOYOS' poetry has been translated into five languages and her work has appeared in the *Longman Anthology of World Literature by Women* (Longman Press), *Mexican American Literature* (Harcourt, Brace, Jovanovich), and *The Third Woman: Minority Women Writers of the United States* (Houghton Mifflin). Her book of poetry is *Woman, Woman* (Arte Público Press). She lives in San Antonio, Texas.

MARTÍN ESPADA is the author of three books of poetry, *The Immigrant Iceboy's Bolero* (Waterfront Press), *Trumpets from the Islands of Their Eviction* (Bilingual Review Press), and *Rebellion Is the Circle of a Lover's Hands* (Curbstone Press). He was awarded the first PEN/Revson Prize in Poetry and has received poetry fellowships from the National Endowment for the Arts and the Massachusetts Arts Council. His work is included in *Under 35: The New Generation of American Poets* (Doubleday/Anchor Books). He is a practicing lawyer in Boston, Massachusetts.

ALICIA GASPAR DE ALBA is the recipient of a 1989 Massachusetts Artists Fellowship and one of three Chicana poets included in the anthology, *Three Times a Woman* (Bilingual Review Press). Her first book of short stories, *The Mystery of Survival*, will appear from Bilingual Review Press in 1992. She is a graduate student in American Studies at the University of New Mexico in Albuquerque.

REBECCA GONZALES is the author of *Flesh and Blood* (Prickly Pear Press), a book of poetry, and teaches high school journalism in Garfield, Texas.

RAY GONZÁLEZ is the editor of six anthologies, including *Crossing the River: Poets of the Western U.S.* (Permanent Press), *Tracks in the Snow: Essays by Colorado Poets* (Mesilla Press), and the forthcoming *The Texas Poetry Anthology* (Corona Press) and *Without Discovery: A Native Response to Columbus* (Broken Moon Press). He is the author of two books of poetry, *From the Restless Roots* (Arte Público Press), and *Twilights and Chants* (James Andrews & Co.,) . He received a 1988 Four Corners Book Award in Poetry, a Colorado Governors Award for Excellence in the Arts, and a Creative Fellowship in Prose from the Colorado Arts Council. He is the Literature Director at the Guadalupe Cultural Arts Center in San Antonio, Texas.

VÍCTOR HERNÁNDEZ CRUZ is the author of six books of poetry, *Snaps* (Vintage Books), *Mainland* (Random House), *Tropicalization* (Reed, Cannon & Johnson), *Bilingual Wholes* (Momos Press), *Rhythm, Content, and*

Flavor (Arte Público Press), and *Red Beans* (Coffee House Press). He lives in Puerto Rico.

JUAN FELIPE HERRERA is the author of numerous books of poetry, including *Facegames* (As Is/So and So Press) and *Akrilica* (Alcatraz Editions). He received a Before Columbus Foundation American Book Award in poetry and a National Endowment for the Arts fellowship. He teaches in the Chicano Studies Program at Fresno State University in Fresno, California.

RITA MAGDALENO has had poetry published in *Pulpsmith, Tonantzin, The Brown Review, Fennel Stalk,* and other journals. She has lived overseas and taught for the European Division of the University of Maryland and presently teaches at Pima Community College in Tucson, Arizona. She is completing her first book of poetry, *Because Our Lives Are Ordinary.*

DEMETRIA MARTÍNEZ is one of three women poets featured in the anthology, *Three Times a Woman* (Bilingual Review Press). She was a reporter for the *Albuquerque Journal* for several years and now writes for the *Catholic Register* in Kansas City, Missouri.

VÍCTOR MARTÍNEZ received a John MacCarron New Writing in Arts Criticism Grant for a book of essays on Chicano/Latino artists and poets he is writing. His work has appeared in *El Tecolote Literario, Zyzzyva, Five Fingers Review, Quarry West, The Iowa Review,* and other journals. His first book of poetry is forthcoming from Chusma Press. He lives in San Francisco.

PAT MORA is the author of three books of poetry from Arte Público Press, *Chants, Borders,* and *Journeys.* The first two books received a Southwest Book Award from the Border Regional Library Assocation. She is also the author of *Tomás and the Library Lady* (Alfred A. Knopf), a children's book. She lives in Cincinnati, Ohio.

JUDITH ORTIZ COFER is the author of a chapbook, *Peregrina* (River-stone Press), a full-length collection of poetry, *Terms of Survival*, and a book of essays, *Silent Dancing: A Partial Remembrance of a Puerto Rican Childhood*, both published by Arte Público Press. Her first novel, *Line of the Sun*, was published by the University of Georgia Press in 1989. She has received poetry fellowships from the National Endowment for the Arts, the Florida Fine Arts Council, and the Witter Bynner Foundation for Poetry. She lives in Athens, Georgia.

LEROY QUINTANA is the author of *Hijo del Pueblo* (Puerto del Sol Press) and has received a National Endowment for the Arts fellowship in poetry. His second book of poetry is forthcoming from Bilingual Review Press. He teaches at Mesa College in San Diego, California.

ANTONIA QUINTANA PIGÑO is the author of the full-length epic poem, "La Jornada," which appeared in a fine-press, limited edition from Zaubergerg Press. She is also the author of a chapbook, *Poesías de 'La Jornado'* (Esoterica Press). Her work has appeared in *Writer's Forum, The Bloomsbury Review, The Kansas Quarterly*, and other journals. She lives in Lawrence, Kansas.

NAOMI QUIÑÓNEZ is the author of a book of poems called *Hummingbird Dreams* and was co-editor of *Multicultural L.A.: An Anthology of Urban Poetry*, both published by West End Press. The latter book received a 1991 Before Columbus Foundation American Book Award. She lives in Los Angeles, California.

ALBERTO RÍOS received the 1982 Walt Whitman Prize in Poetry for his first book, *Whispering to Fool the Wind* (Sheep Meadow Press). His other books of poetry from Sheep Meadow are *Five Indiscretions* and *The Lime Orchard Woman*. His most recent collection of poetry is *Teodoro Luna's Two Kisses* (W. W. Norton). He was given a Western States Book Award in fiction for his book of short stories, *The Iguana Killer* (Confluence Press) in 1984. He teaches at Arizona State University in Tempe.

LUIS J. RODRÍGUEZ is a poet, journalist, and critic whose work has appeared in *The Nation*, *Los Angeles Weekly*, *Americas Review*, and other publications. He received the 1989 Poetry Center Book Award of San Francisco State University for his first book of poems, *Poems Across the Pavement* (Tía Chucha Press). His second book of poetry, *The Concrete River*, was published by Curbstone Press in 1991. He lives in Chicago.

LEO ROMERO is the owner of Books and More Books, a bookstore in Santa Fe, New Mexico. He is the author of several books of poetry, including *During the Growing Season* and *Desert Nights*, from Maguey Press, *Celso* (Arte Público Press), and two books from Ahsahta Press, *Agua Negra* and *Going Home Away*.

BENJAMIN SÁENZ is a native of Las Cruces, New Mexico. His first book of poetry, *Calendar of Dust*, was published in 1991 by Broken Moon Press. His work has appeared in *The Río Grande Review*, *The Seattle Review*, *Puerto del Sol*, *Sequoia*, and other journals. He was a 1988–90 Wallace E. Stegner fellow in poetry at Stanford University. He teaches in the new bilingual MFA Program at the University of Texas in El Paso.

LUIS OMAR SALINAS is the author of numerous books of poetry, including *Crazy Gypsy*, *Afternoon of the Unreal*, *Prelude to Darkness*, *Walking Behind the Spanish*, and *The Sadness of Days: Selected Poems* (Arte Público Press). He has received the Stanley Kunitz Award, the Earl Lyon Award, and the General Electric Foundation Literary Award. He lives in Sanger, California.

GARY SOTO is the author of seven poetry collections. The four published by University of Pittsburgh Press include *The Elements of San Joaquín*, *The Tale of Sunlight*, *Where Sparrows Work Hard*, *and Black Hair*. Scholastic Books published *A Fire in My Hands* in 1989. *Who Will Know Us?* and *Learning Religion* were published in Chronicle Books' new poetry series in 1990–91. He teaches Chicano Studies and English at the University of California at Berkeley.

CARMEN TAFOLLA is the author of several books of poetry, including *Curandera* (MandA Editions) and has written several books of multicultural literature for children. She served as assistant to the president at Northern Arizona University for several years and recently moved back to her native Texas, now living in McAllen.

ERNESTO TREJO studied in the writing program at Fresno State University and also spent time studying poetry in Mexico. His first book of poetry, *Entering a Life*, was published by Arte Público Press in 1990. He died in 1991.

ROBERT VASQUEZ spent two-years as a Wallace E. Stegner Fellow in Poetry at Stanford University. He has been awarded several Academy of American Poets Prizes, and in 1991 his still unpublished manuscript, *At the Rainbow*, received the San Francisco Foundation's James D. Phelan award. His work has appeared in *The Los Angeles Times Book Review*, *The Missouri Review*, *Ploughshares*, *The Village Voice*, and other journals. He lives in Visalia, California, where he teaches at the College of the Sequoias.

ALMA LUZ VILLANUEVA was awarded a Before Columbus Foundation American Book Award for her first novel, *The Ultraviolet Sky* (Bilingual Review Press). Her second novel, *Naked Ladies*, is scheduled to appear from the same publisher in 1991. She is also the author of several books of poetry, including *Bloodroot* and *Life Span* from Place of Herons Press. She lives in Santa Cruz, California.

TINO VILLANUEVA is the publisher of *Imagine: An International Chicano Journal*, one of the oldest Chicano literary magazines in the country. He is the author of several books of poetry, including *Shaking Off the Dark* (Arte Público Press). He teaches at Boston University in Massachusetts. His poems come from a full-length unpublished manuscript, *Scene from the Movie "Giant."*

Acknowledgments

Grateful acknowledgment is made to the following for permission to reprint material copyrighted or controlled by them:

FRANCISCO ALARCÓN and Chronicle Books for "In a Neighborhood in Los Angeles," "Prayer," "My Hair," and "Letter to America" from *Body in Flames*, © 1990 by Francisco Alarcón. Used by permission of the author and publisher.

JIMMY SANTIAGO BACA and New Directions Publishing for "Bells," "Fall," "Day's Blood," and "At Night" from *Black Mesa Poems*, © 1989 by Jimmy Santiago Baca. Used by permission of the author and publisher.

CORDELIA CANDELARIA and Maize Press for "Teenage Son," "Killers," and "Refuse of Our Teeming Shores" from *Ojo de la Cueva*, © 1984 by Cordelia Candelaria. Used by permission of the author and publisher.

ANA CASTILLO for "Nani Worries About Her Father's Happiness in the Afterlife" and "Seduced by Natassja Kinski," © 1990 by Ana Castillo. "Seduced by Natassja Kinski" originally appeared in *Soujourner: The Women's Forum*. Ana Castillo and West End Press for "An Ugly Black Dog Named Goya" and "Zoila López" from *My Father Was a Toltec*, © 1986 by Ana Castillo. Used by permission of the author and publisher.

ROSEMARY CATACALOS and Tooth of Time Books for "One Man's Family" from *Again for the First Time*, © 1984 by Rosemary Catacalos. Used by permission of the author and publisher. Rosemary Catacalos for "A Partial History of Poppies," "The Measure of Light at the Altar of the Day of the Dead," "The Lesson in 'A Waltz for Debby,'" and "With the Conchero Dancers, Mission Espada, July," © 1990 by Rosemary Catacalos. "A Partial History of Poppies" and "The Measure of Light at the Altar of the Day of the Dead" appeared in *The Bloomsbury Review*. "The Lesson in 'A Waltz for Debby'" appeared in *The Cimmarron Review*. "With the Conchero Dancers, Mission Espada, July" appeared in *The Southwest Review*. Used by permission of the author.

LORNA DEE CERVANTES for "A las Gatas," "The Levee: Letter to No One," "Night Stand," and "Drawings for John Who Said to Write About True Love," © 1990 by Lorna Dee Cervantes. "A las Gatas" appeared in *Humanizarte*. "The Levee: Letter to No One" appeared in *Frontiers*. "Drawings for John Who Said to Write About True Love" appeared in *Zyzzyva*. Used by permission of the author.

LUCHA CORPI and Third Woman Press for "Nineteen," "Mariana," "It's Raining," and "Day's Work" from *Variations on a Storm*, © 1990 by Lucha Corpl. Used by permission of the author and publisher.

CARLOS CUMPIÁN and March/Abrazo Press for "Above Drudgery," "The Survivor: Anishinabe Man," and "Coyote Sun" from *Coyote SUN*, © 1989 by Carlos Cumpián. Used by permission of the author and publisher.

ÁNGELA DE HOYOS for "Look Not to Memories" and "Not Even Because You Have Pearl-White Teeth," © 1990 by Angela de Hoyos. Used by permission of the author.

MARTÍN ESPADA and Curbstone Press for "Bully," "Federico's Ghost," "Jorge the Church Janitor Finally Quits," "Niggerlips," "Two Mexicanos Lynched in Santa Cruz, California, May 3, 1971," and "La Tumba de Buena Ventura Roig" from *Rebellion Is the Circle of a Lover's Hands*, © 1990 by Martín Espada. Used by permission of the author.

REBECCA GONZALES and Prickly Pear Press for "Flesh and Blood," and "To the Newlyweds in the Barrio" from *Flesh and Blood*, © 1984 by Rebecca Gonzales. Used by permission of the author and publisher. "Reading the Sky" and "Superstitions," © 1990 by Rebecca Gonzales. Used by permission of the author.

RAY GONZÁLEZ and Southwest Literary Press for "The Sustenance," "Rattlesnake Dance, Coronado Hills, El Paso, 1966," "Snakeskin," and "Three Snakes, Strawberry Canyon, Berkeley" from *The Heat of Arrivals*, © 1991 by Ray González. Used by permission of the author and publisher.

VÍCTOR HERNÁNDEZ CRUZ and Momo's Press for "Two Guitars" and "Geography of the Trinity Corona" from *By Lingual Wholes*. Used by permission of the author and publisher. Victor Hernández Cruz and Arte Público Press for "Don Arturo Says" and "Invisibility O" from *Rhythm, Content, and Flavor*, © 1989 by Víctor Hernández Cruz. Used by permission of the author.

JUAN FELIPE HERRERA and Alcatraz Editions for "The Boy of Seventeen," "Earth Chorus," and "Water Girl" from *Akrilica*, © 1989 by Juan Felipe Herrera. Used by permission of the author and publisher. Juan Felipe Herrera and As Is/So & So Press for "Pyramid of Supplications" from *Facegames*, © 1984 by Juan Felipe Herrera. Used by permission of the author and publisher. Juan Felipe Herrera for "These Words Are Synonymous, Now," © 1990 by Juan Felipe Herrera. Used by permission of the author.

RITA MAGDALENO for "On the Way to the Reunion," "Rosary," "Fall Reunion," and "On Maricopa Road," © 1990 by Rita Magdaleno. Used by permission of the author. "Maricopa Road" appeared in *Tonantzin*.

DEMETRIA MARTÍNEZ and Bilingual Review Press for "Crossing Over," "Chimayo," "Prologue: Salvadoran Woman's Lament" and "Nativity: For Two Salvadoran Women, 1986–87" from *Three Times a Woman*, © 1989 by Demetria Martínez. Used by permission of the author.

VÍCTOR MARTÍNEZ for "The Ledger," "Furniture," "Shoes," "Some Things Left Unsaid," and "All Is Well," © 1990 by Víctor Martínez. Used by permission of the author. "Some Things Left Unsaid" and "All Is Well" appeared in *Quarry West*.

PAT MORA for "Gentle Communion," "Rituals," "Señora X No More," and "Arte Popular," © 1990 by Pat Mora. Used by permission of the author.

JUDITH ORTIZ COFER for "The Dream of Birth," "The Latin Deli," "Saint Rose of Lima," "Fever," "Vida," and "The Campesino's Lament," © 1990 by Judith Ortiz Cofer. "The Dream of Birth" and "The Campesino's Lament" appeared in *Southern Poetry Review*. "Saint Rose of Lima" appeared in *The Americas Review*. "Fever" appeared in *Passages North*. "Vida" appeared in *Parnassus: Poetry in Review*. Used by permission of the author.

LEROY QUINTANA for "Grandfather Never Wrote a Will," "After Her Husband Died, Doña Carlota Was So Alone," "Grandmother's Father Was Killed by Some Tejanos," and "Granizo," © 1990 by Leroy Quintana. Used by permission of the author.

ANTONIA QUINTANA PIGNO and Zauberberg Press for "La Jornada" from LA JORNADA, © by Antonia Quintana Pigno. Used by permission of the author. Antonia Quintana Pigno and Esoterica Press for "Vicente" from *Poesías de 'la Jornada*,' © 1988 by Antonia Quintana Pigno. Used by permission of the author. Antonia Quintana Pigno and Zauberberg Press for "December's Picture" from *Old Town Bridge*, © 1987 by Antonia Quintana Pigno. Used by permission of the author.

NAOMI QUIÑÓNEZ and West End Press for "Hesitations," "My Shattered Sister," "People of the Harvest," and "America's Wailing Wall" from *Hummingbird Dream*, © 1985 by Naomi Quiñónez and from *Invocation L.A.: Urban Multicultural Poetry*, © 1990 by Naomi Quiñónez. Used by permission of the author and publisher.

ALBERTO RÍOS for "I Would Visit Him in the Corner," "Saints, and Their Care," "The Purpose of Altar Boys," and "Lost on September Trail, 1967," © 1982, 1985, and 1988 by Alberto Ríos, from the books *Five Indiscretions, The Lime Orchard Woman*, and *Whispering to Fool The Wind*, all published by Sheep Meadow Press. Used by permission of the author. Alberto Ríos and W. W. Norton & Co. for "The Good Lunch of Oceans" from *Teodoro Lunas's Two Kisses*, © 1990 by Alberto Ríos. Used by permission of the author and publisher.

LUIS J. RODRÍGUEZ and Tía Chucha Press for "Juchitán" and "Tomatoes" from *Poems Across the Pavement*, © 1989 by Tía Chucha Press. Luis J. Rodgríuez and Curbstone Press for "Every Breath a Prayer" from *The Concrete River*, © 1990 by Luis J. Rodgríguez. Used by permission of the author and publisher.

LEO ROMERO for "If Marilyn Monroe," "Pito, I Say," "Time Is What You Make of It," "In This Dream, Pito And," "In This Dream, I Drop By," © 1990 by Leo Romero. Used by permission of the author. "If Marilyn Monroe" appeared in *The South Dakota Review*.

BENJAMIN SÁENZ and Broken Moon Press for "Resurrections," "Easter," "At Thirteen," "Creation. Trinity Site, New Mexico, 5:30 A.M., July 16th, 1945" from *Calender of Dust*, © 1991 by Benjamin Sáenz. Used by permission of the author and publisher.

LUIS OMAR SALINAS for "Late Evening Conversations with My Friend's Dog, Moses, After Watching Visconti's 'The Innocent,'" "In Mazatlán," "I'm Walking Behind the Spanish," and "I Am America" from *Walking Behind the Spanish*, © 1982 by Luis Omar Salinas. "Crazy Gypsy" from *Crazy Gypsy*, © 1970 by Luis Omar Salinas. "This Is About the Way It Should Be" from *Prelude to Darkness*, © 1981 Luis Omar Salinas. Used by permission of the author.

GARY SOTO and Chronicle Books for "The Seventieth Year," "A Red Palm," "Pink Hands," and "Who Will Know Us?" from *Who Will Know Us?*, © 1990 by Gary Soto. Used by permission of the author and publisher.

CARMEN TAFOLLA for "Hat Line," "La Miss Low," and "Poquito Allá," © 1990 by Carmen Tafolla. Used by permission of the author.

ERNESTO TREJO and Arte Público Press for "The Cloud Unfolding," "Cypriana," "The President Is Up Before the First Vendor," and "For Jaime Sabines" from *Entering a Life*, © 1990 by Ernesto Trejo. Used by permission of the author.

ROBERT VASQUEZ for "Early Morning Test Light Over Nevada, 1955," "Día de los Muertos," "California Sonnets: Night Sequence," and "Coyotes," © 1990 by Robert Vásquez. Used by permission of the author. "Early Morning Test Light Over Nevada, 1955" appeared in *New Voices*. "Día de Los Muertos" appeared in *The New England Review—Middlebury Series*. "Coyotes" appeared in *Ploughshares*. Used by permission of the author.

ALMA LUZ VILLANUEVA and Place of Herons Press for "The Balance" from *Life Span*, © 1985 by Alma Villanueva. Used by permission of the author. Alma Villanueva for "Wolf at the Door," "Things of

Our Childhood," and "Power," © 1990 by Alma Villanueva. Used by permission of the author. "Wolf at the Door" appeared in *The Sun*.

TINO VILLANUEVA for "On the Subject of Staying Whole" and "The Trailing Consequence: A Triptych," © 1990 by Tino Villanueva. Used by permission of the author. "The Trailing Consequence: A Triptych" appeared in *Tinta: Revista de Letras Hispánicas y Luso-Brasileñas*.

258 ▲ ACKNOWLEDGMENTS

After Aztlan

was set in Joanna, one of Eric Gill's least used and most beautiful faces. Probably named after his daughter Joan, it was first used as a proprietary face at the printing press Gill ran with René Hague. Unlike Perpetua, which looks as though it were engraved with a burin, Joanna looks as though it were cut with a chisel; it is heavier and more monotone in its weight. It maintains the typical Perpetua forms, but the serifs are slab sided and the capitals are visibly shorter than the ascenders. Like Perpetua, the italic is really a sloped Roman, but it is highly condensed and decidedly calligraphic in many of its features. Its evenness, density, and readability, and its slightly quirky elegance make Joanna the perfect choice for a book of poetry.

Book design by Lucinda Hitchcock; typesetting by Graphic Composition, Athens, Georgia. Printed and bound by Haddon Craftsmen, Scranton, Pennsylvania.